WHY WORRY?

After taking a degree in psychology at Swansea, Sue Breton stayed in Wales and did her clinical training in the NHS. When her family grew to five children, she left fulltime work to care for them and completed her MA, researching panic attacks. For several years she lectured on psychology and taught stress management at the University Hospital of Wales. She now combines writing self-help psychology books with psychotherapy work, specializing in anxiety-related problems.

Why Worry?

HOW TO STOP WORRYING

AND ENJOY YOUR LIFE

Sue Breton

ELEMENT
Shaftesbury, Dorset ● Rockport, Massachusetts
Brisbane, Queensland

© Sue Breton 1994

First published in Great Britain in 1994 by
Element Books Limited
Shaftesbury, Dorset

Published in the USA in 1994 by
Element, Inc.
42 Broadway, Rockport, MA 01966

Published in Australia by
Element Books Limited for
Jacaranda Wiley Limited,
33 Park Road, Milton, Brisbane, 4064

Cover design by Max Fairbrother
Text design by Roger Lightfoot
Typeset by The Electronic Book Factory Ltd, Fife, Scotland
Printed and bound in Great Britain by
Redwood Books Limited, Trowbridge, Wiltshire

British Library Cataloguing in Publication
data available

Library of Congress Cataloging in publication
data available

ISBN 1–85230–556–8

Contents

Introduction

A woman in her thirties went to see her GP complaining of inability to sleep, restlessness and a general loss of energy. The GP, recognizing the signs and symptoms of stress, questioned the patient about her lifestyle.

He discovered that, although she had a husband and two school-age children to care for, she also had a full-time job in a dry cleaners. Not only that, but in her spare time she was an active committee member of the PTA and secretary of the local darts team.

The GP concluded that the woman was doing too much. Since she had to keep caring for her family, and as she needed the extra income from her job in order to maintain the family's standard of living, the doctor said she should give up her commitments to the PTA and darts team.

For some eighteen months I had been planning to write this book. From time to time I'd earnestly add ideas and anecdotes to my notes, but never actually began the writing. There was always some excuse to put it off a bit longer. The very same day I heard the above story, I slotted a new disk into the word processor and began.

'How is this book different?' I hear you cry. 'Every bookshop already displays several different versions of overcoming anxiety, of living with stress, and so on. Do we need another?'

My answer to this is obviously, 'Yes'. I'll explain why.

Have you ever tried to learn something, had it explained to you several times, but you still couldn't grasp it? Then, one day, someone explains it again but perhaps using slightly different words and, all at once, the penny drops and you wonder why it had seemed so hard to understand before.

One occasion I still recall vividly when this happened to me was when I was learning to drive. I never seemed to know precisely when and why I should change gear. My instructor explained again and again. Sometimes I thought I'd understood, but then, when I tried to put it into practice, I'd realize I hadn't understood at all.

One day a friend, who was accompanying me for a practice drive, said the same thing my instructor always said, but used different words, different pictures . . . and all at once I knew I understood!

In clinical practice I have often repeated explanations, in different forms, to the same person on different occasions. I no longer mind having to do this because I accept now that sooner or later I will hit upon the most meaningful way of saying it to this particular person, and the effort will all have been worthwhile.

Thus, some books on anxiety and stress control will suit some people, whereas others may use a different approach that will suit others. My justification, therefore, for producing yet another book on this subject is simply that I'm giving another viewpoint – one which has been tested in clinical situations with people whose anxiety and stress varies from the slight to the very severe. So how is my way different?

I expect you know of many people, maybe even yourself, who've been told to take it easy, to slow down, to do less. Usually, it's what's most enjoyable that has to be pruned away. Is there any wonder that much of this advice goes unheeded? There are numerous jokes based on the advice that, by avoiding parties, over-eating, and other forms of debauchery, you may live to a ripe old age – only to die of boredom!

All too often modern medicine, in its obsession with the quantity of life, neglects its quality. Francis Bacon, the great statesman and philosopher of the late sixteenth century, observed, 'Cure the disease and kill the patient.'

The advice given in the story at the start of this book overlooked the psychological factors. Those aspects of the patient's life which she was advised to forego were probably the very things which made her life worthwhile.

My message is that where worry, stress and anxiety are the problem, you don't have to give up what you enjoy in order to overcome them.

Worry, stress and anxiety can indeed provoke physical illnesses. But if the cause is psychological, the 'cure' must be too. Although the resulting physical symptoms, for example, ulcers and heart attacks, may be treated by physical methods, the psychological cause often remains. The psychologically sound 'cure' for such disorders is not boredom or even depression, as must often be the consequence of much advice to sufferers.

Over the years, having been confronted with such problems in the course of my work, I have accumulated a repertoire of approaches to treatment for all kinds of people with widely varying needs. It is my intention here to set out a psychologically sound approach to coping with stress, worry and anxiety. An approach which can be used by anyone, whatever their circumstances, and which, in many cases, does away with the very limited choice of either a long life or a happy one. My aim is to show how it may be possible to have both!

It is an approach which parents can instil in their children to help them grow up less anxiety and stress prone than their elders.

'What's the catch?' you ask.

Well, obviously, psychology cannot remove irreversible physical damage already caused by stress-related disorders. For instance, it cannot make a damaged heart as good as new. But, in such cases, it can help the sufferer come happily to terms with physical limitations, so as not to increase the damage.

The second 'catch' is that an enjoyable stress-free lifestyle isn't necessarily either quick or easy to achieve. Patience, motivation, and an open mind are basic requirements. But, given these, it isn't hard.

The book is divided into two parts. The first part examines worry, stress and anxiety, and attempts to explain what they are. It then helps the reader understand precisely how this applies to him or her. There is a 'Lesson in Understanding' at the end of each chapter in Part One to help with this.

The second part describes ways in which the reader may begin to change and move towards the goal of a better life.

At the end of each chapter in Part Two a specific exercise in 'Positive Living' is suggested.

Real-life case histories are used throughout to add interest and to show readers that others have had their problems too (the identities of the people concerned have been changed).

This book attempts to lead readers towards ways of breathing new meaning and purpose into our life on Earth. It will be of benefit to almost everyone.

In modern western societies, our ordinary way of life is stress-inducing. Our lifestyle may have moved on from our cave-dwelling days, but our emotional reactions haven't. Thus many of them are now inappropriate and as a result cause us problems.

In order to understand where we go wrong, it is helpful to look back to early man and our basic instinctive behaviours for clues as to the original reasons for our behaviour today. Once we understand our behaviour and responses, we can reshape them and update them so as to help our survival today.

If my explanations seem, at times, oversimplified or even childish, I make no apologies for this. I frequently use mental images because our brains generally remember best in terms of simple pictures, rather than in flowing prose.

The aim of this book is to show you how to teach your mind new habits. The most efficient way of doing this is by flashing pictures into it, much as you might do with a slide projector onto a screen. Hopefully, each picture you flash onto the screen of your mind will already have some special meaning – probably one of greater control or calm.

The simplest ways are often the best.

How do you see life?

I suggest that before you read any further you keep a diary for anything from two days to a week. The purpose of this is to help you to see more clearly exactly how the ways you view the world at present could be improved. In Chapter 8 you will be asked to refer to this diary and consider what you've written.

The diary must contain your thoughts and feelings about what happens, or doesn't happen, to you over the period in question. It need not include every tiny detail of your life, simply those events about which you have strong feelings.

Below is a fictitious example of one day's entry for Calamity Jane.

Friday 13 May

Everything went wrong today as I expected! In the first place I overslept. Then, on the way to work, I was rushing because I was going to be late. I mounted the pavement at one point to go round a car that was taking a long time making a right turn. As I put my two inside wheels up on the kerb, I ran over a broken milk bottle. Really! People should be more careful about things like that, it's disgusting the way rubbish is just thrown around anywhere. Anyhow, the broken glass punctured my front tyre.

I found the spare in the boot but I didn't want to lift it out because it would make my skirt dirty. I stood there for a while wondering what to do. I thought I'd call the breakdown service, but then realized they'd take ages to get there and then I'd really be late for work.

Of course nobody else bothered to stop and help, selfish lot! In the end I tried to lift the spare from the boot and laddered my tights. Now I knew I'd really look a mess by the time I got to work, and I'd be very late.

Anyway, in the end I left the car and caught a bus. When I got to work I phoned the garage and asked them to collect the car. They brought it to me later in the day – along with a bill. At lunchtime, to make matters worse, the cafeteria didn't have any curry. It was the kind of day when I'd really fancied curry. I had to have some new stuff, lasagne I think it was. Not bad.

By the time I got home that night I was longing for a hot bath but I found I'd forgotten to switch on the immersion heater that morning and the water was cold. What a disaster! The next Friday 13th I'm going to stay in bed!

PART ONE

Understanding Worry and Negative Arousal

CHAPTER ONE

Fear – Anxiety – Stress – Worry – Guilt

Mary, an ample lady of advancing years, entered my office and deposited herself on the armchair beside the desk. The armchair let out a sigh as she sank onto it, but Mary didn't. She remained rigid in posture, her eyes fixed on my face.

I'd had a referral letter from her GP but wanted to know what she considered her problem to be, so I asked.

She looked straight at me. 'I worry,' she said.

'But what do you worry about?'

'Everything.'

'Such as what? Give me some examples.'

Mary thought for a moment. 'Like my daughter's marriage.'

'I see. And why do you worry about your daughter's marriage?'

At this point she frowned as if unable to understand why I should ask such an obvious question. Then, as if addressing a slow-witted child, she continued, 'In case they split up or anything.'

'And how does your worry help?' I persisted gently.

Now she seemed really at a loss for words. She thought hard for several seconds but couldn't seem to find an answer.

'Does your worry solve the problem?' I prompted.

'No ... but ...'

'Then why do you worry?'

That question was easier, it seemed. She straightened her

back, crossed her arms and, looking me straight in the eye, announced, 'I have to worry to show I care!'

Further probing revealed that Mary had worried herself into a corner. Because she worried so much and raised her blood pressure, the family had taken to not telling her their troubles in order to protect her health. She, on the other hand, was a highly perceptive person – as worriers are – and could detect when something was amiss. Her family's tactics only served to increase her worry because not only did she worry about what the problem might be, she also worried about how she could get the family to tell her the truth about whatever it was!

This true story demonstrates several important points where worry is concerned and I shall return to it often throughout the book.

You may not identify with Mary directly. You may be young, slim, male ... but the fact that you're reading this probably indicates you have much in common with her, as do an extremely high proportion of the population of the developed world.

We are constantly told today that worry and stress are major causes of physical illness. The majority of people, if asked, would no doubt reply that worry, stress and similar emotions are bad for us. On balance they'd be right.

When humans were created, the ability to be afraid was given them for a purpose. In this chapter I hope to be able to show the difference between fear, anxiety, stress, worry, and guilt. Throughout Part One I shall attempt to explain the part played by each of these emotions in our lives today compared to the part each was intended to play.

In Part Two I shall describe various tried and tested ways that you can help yourself shape the part played by those emotions to that which nature, rather than modern living, intended.

Before we turn to anxiety and its variations, let us begin with the response nature gave us to ensure we kept out of harm's way – fear.

FEAR

Fear is an unpleasant emotion which we have when threatened. A response that could be construed as fear has been observed in almost all living creatures.

Consider for a moment. If you have a pet, can you tell when it's afraid? Can you tell when your child's afraid? Of course you can. You also, no doubt, recognize fear in yourself.

Fear may be expressed in different ways but, used properly, it serves an essential life-saving purpose. Note that I said, 'used properly'. Unlike other living creatures, man has developed the ability to abuse fear. Worry, stress, anxiety, apprehension, and many similar emotions are all variations of the basic fear response.

In order to understand how we abuse fear, let us first look at its true life-saving purpose . . . When the brain feels fear it triggers particular bodily reactions. First, the heartbeat becomes faster and stronger, allowing the oxygen carried in the blood to be distributed more rapidly throughout the body. We've all noticed the way our hearts begin to thump when we become afraid. The blood supply to the skin is temporarily diverted, going instead to the muscles and brain where it's needed to support the extra effort. This causes the skin to grow paler – the white face associated with fear. Breathing deepens in order to take in the greater amounts of oxygen demanded by the other functions. Hence the 'gasping' sensation some people feel when afraid.

As well as these observable happenings, other reactions occur, unseen, within the body. For example, the liver releases sugar to be used by the muscles. There's an increase in the ability of the blood to clot.

Why do all these physiological reactions occur? Why does the body suddenly demand this extra oxygen, this release of sugar to the muscles, and so on?

If we consider ourselves in our more primitive days, the answer is obvious. Prehistoric man, when confronted by a large hairy mammoth, could do one of two things. He could either run (flight) or stand his ground and attempt to defend himself (fight). In order to do either, increased physical exertion would be required.

At the first glimpse of the mammoth his brain received the message that he was afraid. The brain responded, as ours still do today, by preparing the body for physical action – for flight or for fighting (see Figure 1).

This reaction to fear has been termed the emergency reaction – the way we react in an emergency. In modern life, however, where attack by a hairy mammoth is rare, this physical response to our fear is often either unnecessary or too late.

Have you ever narrowly missed an accident of some kind, to find just afterwards that you're showing all the symptoms of the flight or fight response? Have you almost broken a prized ornament when dusting, reacted automatically and caught it as it fell, then had to sit down because your heart was pounding? Have you ever stepped into the road without looking and just managed to jump back again before a passing bus flattened you, only to find yourself panting and your heart thumping?

It is easy, then, to understand the evolutionary purpose of this bodily reaction to fear in the face of an immediate threat. In the three examples above, the reaction to danger was automatic, that is, it wasn't planned. It happened instinctively. For the body to have reacted so quickly it first had to be set in motion by the brain.

This type of reaction usually works well in most of us *in the right circumstances*. Modern living, however, rarely permits the flight response. We don't always find ourselves able to run away from what's scaring us. When the need to run away is blocked or prevented for some reason, the fear often turns into aggression instead. Most animals will, when afraid, choose flight first. If this isn't possible, they turn to fight instead. Think of pets you've owned. Wouldn't they prefer to run from danger if they could?

If you are a parent, have you never found yourself shouting angrily at a child of yours that you've just watched narrowly avoid serious injury?

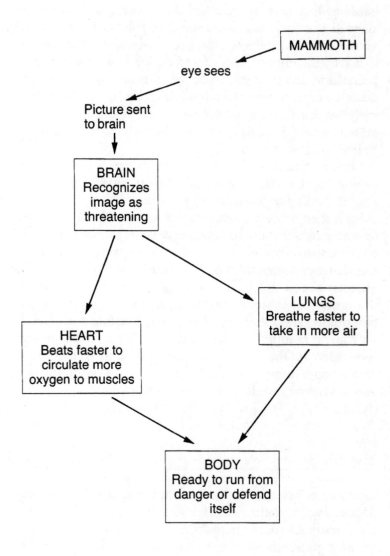

Figure 1: Man's Instinctive Reaction to Danger

One day I was with my children, waiting at a pelican crossing for the green man to flash. I assumed the children were doing the same, having had it drummed into them from babyhood. A man approached the crossing in a hurry and stepped out to cross, dodging the traffic as he went. One of my children, thinking the man had crossed because the lights had changed, stepped off the kerb without looking. I saw him go and, in a split second, looked up and saw a car heading straight for him. Mercifully, he too noticed it just in time and ran back to safety. Whereupon I found myself, heart pounding, chastising him angrily. The child was frightened and crying.

My reaction wasn't intended as a punishment. It was simply my own fear response, set off when I'd seen the danger, finding an outlet in aggression.

Fear, then, is the emotion set off by the brain in the face of an immediate threat and to which the body responds by preparing for flight or fight. When the brain signals the danger's over, the body resumes normal service. The physical action involved in fleeing or fighting has used up the provisions made for it by the increased oxygen intake, blood flow, and other chemical changes within the body.

'Wait a minute!' I hear you say. 'What if we haven't responded to the fear by actually running or fighting or venting our feelings through aggression?' A very good point, and a very important one. I shall return to it later in this chapter.

ANXIETY

First we must consider a third possible response to fear – that of 'freezing'. Sometimes a frightened animal doesn't move at all. It becomes totally immobile.

This type of reaction seems to occur when the creature isn't really certain of the nature of the threat. It's as if it's biding its time, perhaps hoping the threat will pass. Because the threat is less immediate, there isn't the need for such instant action.

A rabbit, enjoying a meal of carrot tops in a farmer's field one night, notices an owl some way off. The rabbit doesn't run, not until it actually knows the owl has seen it. Instead, it remains motionless, as if trying not to draw attention to itself in the hope that the owl will find something else to eat.

In our modern world, most of the threats we encounter are of this kind – psychological rather than physical in origin. They are fears of what *might* happen rather than of what is actually happening.

Although the motor car represents a physical threat, we know that, unlike the hairy mammoth, it won't harm us as long as we keep out of its way. Although unforeseen accidents with cars do occur, they don't generally provoke anxiety *before* the event simply because they are *unforeseen*. (There are exceptions to this in people who have developed phobias as a result of unforeseen experiences, but I shall return to these in Chapter 2.)

On the whole, therefore, anxiety is an emotion caused by a foreseeable threat and the preparation of the individual to face that threat. It is anxiety that most people feel when waiting outside an examination room – anxiety as to whether they know enough, whether they'll remember all they should.

This is just one example. We may have other anxieties stemming from worries over the future, ranging from concerns over whether we'll have a job next year to what others might think of us if we inadvertently wear the wrong clothes to a coming social function.

Although the emotion is anxiety rather than fear, the body responds similarly to both. As the anxiety increases, so the physical symptoms become stronger. If the threat becomes real fairly rapidly and passes, the anxiety dies away, as does fear. Nevertheless, as with fear, the body's preparations are often not used.

This type of anxiety does have a beginning and an end. It begins when the person becomes aware of the impending unpleasant event, and should end when that event is over. In many instances this kind of anxiety is useful to us, as I shall explain in the next chapter.

STRESS

Then there's stress. Stress is a kind of endless anxiety. Hans Selye[1] explained the mechanism of stress in terms of his General Adaptation Syndrome (GAS). This has three stages.

The first stage is alarm. In this stage the mind and body react to a threat in the same way as they do with fear. With stress, however, the threat doesn't pass so the alarm reaction remains. The effect on the body may be compared to that of waiting in the car at traffic lights with the clutch raised to 'biting' point so the car is poised to move when the lights turn green. When the lights turn green, the threat is removed and the car moves off, relieved. If, however, the lights stick on red, the car keeps churning, but going nowhere. Eventually this would burn out the clutch and take its toll on the engine. A similar process occurs in humans in the face of unrelieved stress.

The second stage of the GAS is resistance. Because it is in a state of ongoing anxiety the body's physical response is tiring it out. In order to conserve its energy, it shuts down other systems temporarily in order to conserve its resources. For instance, sexual and reproductive behaviour is often terminated.

Humans under stress frequently lose interest in sex. In women, periods may stop or become very erratic. In men there is often a fall in the production of spermatozoa. People who are over-anxious to have children have often been known to become infertile simply from the wanting. It used to be quite common for a childless couple to adopt a baby and then for the woman to become pregnant herself.

The final stage is exhaustion. If the stress continues unabated, the body reaches a point where it finds itself no longer able to function even on reduced power as it has been and total shut-down results. This can be either a physical collapse or a mental collapse – often in the form of an acute anxiety state or depressive illness. This is the 'nervous breakdown' of which the layman speaks.

WORRY

For now, I want to consider the third form of this type of response – worry.

The 'worry' of Mary at the start of this chapter is a case in point. Worry is that emotion which we have when we feel anxiety over events and outcomes which we have no power to influence. The roots of worry usually lie in our attempts to control something or someone within our world. For instance, we fret over how to get a difficult colleague at work to do as they should, how to make a teenager dress the way we consider they should, how to persuade a stubborn elderly relative to change their way of life for their own benefit . . .

Worry is often regarded as the layman's name for anxiety and, in many instances, this is the case. Personally, however, I prefer to save the label 'worry' for the kind of anxiety which serves no useful purpose. 'If you're not worried then you should be!' Was that ever said to you as a child – by one of your parents or by a teacher? Have you ever found yourself saying it?

In my experience it's used most often as a threat. For instance, with school exams looming, a child does bad work and is given that warning. What is actually meant is that if more effort isn't made, the exam won't be passed. What the teacher really means to say is, 'Come on, get motivated!' The word 'worry' isn't necessary – just as worry itself isn't. You need to be motivated to do well in an exam but you don't need to be motivated by worry.

In some cases worry is similar to the freezing reaction to danger observed in animals. I have known people who became so locked into worrying about what might happen that they were powerless to take action they should have been taking (more about this later.)

GUILT

Guilt is the aftermath. It only occurs when an event is over. It happens when we recall something we've done and wish we'd done it differently, or over something we didn't do that we wish we had. Deep guilt can produce symptoms similar to those of severe anxiety.

Whereas fear and anxiety are similar because they are both short-lived experiences, so worry, guilt and stress are the long-term equivalents. To my mind, worry only differs from stress insofar as the causes of the worry are such that the worrier has no power over them.

The body reacts to all five with physiological changes. In the cases of fear and anxiety these generally die away once the threat has passed, leaving no permanent damage. Since the body's reactions are designed to promote physical activity, the fear and anxiety often fade quicker if the person has undertaken some kind of active movement – such as running.

The consequences of worry, guilt and stress are more serious. Apart from nervous breakdowns, the various chemical changes produced in the body during long-lasting anxiety may lead to various physical diseases such as ulcers and heart attacks. Such conditions are often referred to as 'stress-induced diseases' for this very reason.

Stress and worry in modern life are not, as some would have us believe, inevitable. They are not so much a product of modern lifestyles as of modern ways of thinking.

It is possible to adapt to modern life so as to survive it. Our ancestors no doubt adapted their lives so as to avoid physical threats to life and limb from marauding creatures. If they hadn't done so, they'd have become extinct. Equally, we must adapt our lives so as to avoid psychological threats if we're to survive and enjoy it.

SUMMARY

Before proceeding to the next chapter, let us once more look at our definitions.

FEAR – the body's survival response to an immediate threat.

ANXIETY – the mind and body's response to a less immediate

threat, but a threat which the person has the power to terminate.

STRESS – endless anxiety or worry to which the mind and body keep reacting because the cause is unresolved.

WORRY – the same response as anxiety but to a threat which the person can exert no influence over.

GUILT – the same response as anxiety but to something which has passed.

The ways in which I've defined fear, anxiety, stress, worry and guilt in this chapter are my own. You may find these terms used differently in other books. But the names aren't really important in themselves, they're a means to an end.

My aim is to help you to understand the differences between the causes of each and the feelings and thoughts that underlie them. Don't become upset or angry if you're slightly confused at this point – the aim of the book is to lead you to an understanding by the end of it. Figure 2 on p.20 may help to clarify these differences. I've presented Trog, the caveman, in certain situations and showed his thoughts at the time, and labelled them accordingly.

LESSON ONE IN UNDERSTANDING

If you wish, you can further test your understanding so far by reading the following descriptions and attempting to label the emotion involved. Is it fear, anxiety, stress, worry, or guilt in each case? The answers and an explanation are given at the end in Appendix I.

1. You're taking an exam tomorrow, the outcome of which is very important for you. You feel agitated, unable to settle. You want to relax and attempt to watch TV but you can't seem to get into the programmes . . .

Is this . . . fear/anxiety/stress/worry/guilt?

2. Your daughter is taking her driving test this morning. You go about your business as best you can but with a

churning inside you and a wish that you could be doing it for her . . .

Is this . . . fear/anxiety/stress/worry/guilt?

3. You dislike heights. You're watching a TV programme in which the goodie and the baddie are fighting on the edge of a precipice. Your toes curl up, your hands grip the arms of your chair, your heartbeat increases . . .

Is this fear/anxiety/stress/worry/guilt?

4. Your husband has told you that there's a real possibility he'll be made redundant in three months time. Although nothing's definite, you can't put the thought from your mind. You wonder constantly whether the redundancy pay will be enough for your commitments. You're unable to do anything positive, your short-term memory becomes erratic so you find yourself forgetting things at the shops, etc.

SITUATION	THOUGHT	FEELING
Trog the caveman sees mammoth	'It's going to kill me. I can't escape!'	FEAR
Trog bids mother goodbye as he goes to find food	'I hope I don't meet a mammoth today!'	ANXIETY
Trog thinks as he lies in bed at night	'I wish I didn't have to go hunting every day. Suppose I meet a mammoth and can't escape?	STRESS
Mrs Trog sits in cave biting nails and not getting laundry done	'I hope Trog doesn't meet a mammoth today!'	WORRY

Figure 2

Is this fear/anxiety/stress/worry/guilt?

5. You have just dented another car whilst parking in front of it. As you survey the damage you notice a man, presumably the other car's owner, approaching rapidly with a none-too-friendly expression on his face. Your heart beats faster, your mouth goes dry . . .

Is this fear/anxiety/stress/worry/guilt?

6. You had a very bad row with someone at work yesterday. When everyone had gone home you found that you were in the wrong after all. You intend to apologize the next day. The next morning, however, you discover that the colleague to whom you owe the apology died of a heart attack during the night. Over the next few weeks you grow more and more uncomfortable, unable to make decisions or concentrate . . .

Is this fear/anxiety/stress/worry/guilt?

CHAPTER TWO

Sentry Duty

In the previous chapter I attempted to explain the body's reaction to anxiety-type emotions. Now it is time to consider the part played by the brain. Exactly how and why do our thoughts turn to fear and anxiety when they do?

Professor Jeffrey Gray[2] has come up with a very good explanation based upon what he calls the 'Behavioural Inhibition System'. The whole theory is very complex. However, in my clinical work I have found my simplified version immensely useful as a means of explaining to people how their anxiety comes about. I call it 'Sentry Duty' and you'll soon see why.

Why is it that:

- If you live beside a busy main road you aren't kept awake at night by the traffic, whereas your guests may well be?
- If you're used to sleeping in towns you can't get to sleep in the peaceful countryside?
- You often feel slightly uneasy when you have to wear the kind of clothes you don't normally wear?

You might say that the answer to all these questions is, 'It depends what you're used to.' And you'd be right. But how does not being used to something affect us? What is actually happening in our heads? In this context I often recall something which used to happen to me as a teenager.

I was very fond of pop music, but never listened to the

classics. I used to hear occasional pieces of light classical music on the radio and my piano teacher made me learn to play pieces by Beethoven from time to time. But that was all.

At school, however, were several girls who came from musical backgrounds, or whose parents had taught them from an early age to appreciate the classics. It soon became obvious that a knowledge of classical music was highly approved of at my school and so, wanting to be approved of, I decided I should broaden my own tastes. Some evenings, when my parents were out, I'd stop playing my usual accompaniment of pop and put a classical record on instead. I'd then attempt to follow the piece through the different stages as we'd been taught at school.

This wasn't too bad for about an hour or so, but then I'd begin to feel what I used to describe to myself as 'strange'. I now know that these feelings of 'strangeness' were, in fact, anxiety.

When this feeling came upon me I'd have to stop playing the classical record. I'd replace it with my favourite pop records and sing along to them for ten minutes or so, after which I'd feel 'normal' again.

Not surprisingly, because playing the classical records used to bring on this uncomfortable 'strangeness', I didn't rush to repeat the experience and it would usually be some months before I tried again! Only when, in adult life, I began to remember those evenings in the light of the 'sentry' in my head, did they finally make sense.

We all have a 'sentry' in our heads whose purpose, like those real sentries outside Buckingham Palace, is to stand guard. When everything is running smoothly and normally, the sentry at the palace stands unobtrusively, watching but not doing anything. Only when something out of the ordinary and potentially dangerous occurs, does the sentry swing into action.

The 'sentry' in our heads works in much the same way. At any time when we're awake, a whole mass of information is being picked up by our senses, by touch, by smell, by taste, by hearing, by sight. While you are reading this, for instance, you are doubtless concentrating mainly on what your eyes are picking up as they read the words on the page. You are not consciously aware – until I now point it out to you – of the feel of the book in your hands, the feel of your clothes against your skin, the taste in your mouth, the smell of the room – unless perhaps you're hungry and you're noticing the smell of food wafting from the kitchen, in which case you probably aren't concentrating on what you're reading!

So you see, really we only consciously pay attention to the information being fed through one of our senses at a time unless we make a particular effort to be more aware of the others too. This shutting off from our conscious minds of the information we don't actually require at any one time is what is meant to happen. It enables us to concentrate the power of our brains on what's most important to us at that time.

When some other information reaches us whilst we're concentrating on something else we call it a distraction. Sometimes we merely ignore the unwanted extra information. At other times we deliberately shut it out. For instance, have you ever found yourself closing your eyes in order to hear something more clearly? Have you ever noticed how often people close their eyes when enjoying a pleasant taste or the feel of something special? Under normal circumstances our conscious minds settle on the information we're concentrating on and ignore the rest. Nevertheless, the rest is still picked up by another part of our brains – the sentry.

HOW THE SENTRY WORKS

Imagine you're deeply absorbed in a film you're watching on TV. So deeply absorbed that you just don't consciously hear when another member of the family asks you if you'd like a chocolate. When, however, the cat in the kitchen knocks over a pile of saucepans, making a loud crash, you look up immediately. This is the work of your sentry on duty.

The job of the sentry in your head is to watch and monitor

all that information being fed into your brain from your senses that you're not consciously paying attention to. This is important for our survival as a species.

Think of Trog, the caveman. Suppose Trog went out hunting and became absorbed in watching a beautiful cave-woman take a bath in a stream. If he had no sentry on duty in his head, he could be so oblivious to everything else that he wouldn't notice the hairy mammoth approaching from almost behind him.

But in Trog's case the sentry saves him. It picks up the movements of the mammoth as it approaches and, just as yours might alert you to the crash in the kitchen as the saucepans were knocked over, so Trog's sentry would drag his thoughts away from the cave-woman to concentrate instead on the danger (see Figure 3, p.26).

The sentry, then, watches what's going on around us whilst we're concentrating on something else. How does the sentry know what to draw our attention to and what to ignore?

The sentry learns what is and what isn't dangerous from experience. If you live with a cat that constantly knocks over piles of saucepans with no ill effects, then in all probability your sentry wouldn't draw your attention to the fact, and you'd just carry on watching your film without looking up. It's the possibility of danger that's important to the sentry.

Think of the guard outside Buckingham Palace. He may take no notice of the regular weekly laundry van because the van has proved in past experience to pose no threat. On the other hand, if the van arrives at other than its usual day and time, or if it's a different colour, or has some other unexpected feature, the guard will probably become more watchful and wary, ready for danger. If the new type of van proves to be safe, the guard will eventually take as little notice of it as he does the regular one. If, however, the new van proves to be dangerous, it is likely that if it ever appears again the guard won't merely become more watchful, he'll challenge it immediately!

Thus, it's the way we react to the warnings of our sentries that determines how much notice they'll take of a similar situation in the future. If a strange dog approaches you one day, your sentry may make you extra watchful. If the dog turns out to be friendly, your sentry will record the fact and will probably not raise your awareness the next time you meet it. If, however, the dog bites you, your sentry will mark it down as dangerous and your level of awareness will increase tremendously the next time you meet it, ready for evasive action. This is how many phobias come about.

When the sentry in our heads becomes wary, our level of awareness increases so that we're ready, in the event of a real danger, for the flight or fight response. The more likely the danger appears, the greater the preparation for it. However, once the sentry in your head becomes aware

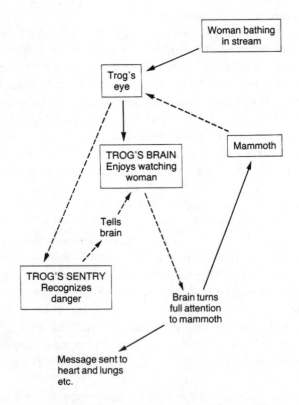

Figure 3: How Trog's Sentry Warns Him

of danger and alerts you to it, it switches your attention to that potential danger making it very hard for you to think of anything else.

Thus, many phobia sufferers find it almost impossible to ignore what they're afraid of because their sentries ensure they keep reacting to it. I shall say more about retraining the sentry in Part 2.

Let me now return to the example I gave of myself and the classical records. Because the sentry in our heads learns from experience, it treats anything new as a potential threat and makes us react accordingly. My sentry wasn't accustomed to listening to classical music. Thus, as I listened I tended to become slightly anxious. I noticed this feeling and decided I didn't like it. My sentry stored my dislike associated with the classical records and the next time I played them it warned me of the potential danger again. Playing pop records used to bring me back to 'normal' and dispel my anxiety because I was used to these and enjoyed them, so my sentry remained quiet.

What can we learn from this about our everyday lives? We must realize that whenever we do something new, no matter what, even going on holiday to unfamiliar surroundings, our sentries will become watchful because they haven't learnt that those places, and those circumstances, are safe. I shall deal in Part 2 with how to overcome the unease that often results from this. For now it is important just to be aware that it happens and why.

Having said that the sentry in our heads learns what is and what isn't dangerous by experience, I must point out that there are some fears which it has instinctively.

INSTINCTIVE FEARS

These appear in every member of a species. They're born into us along with the number of arms and legs we're to have. Human babies, at about the time they start to crawl, show a fear of heights. Horses have an instinctive fear of snakes which, in many of them, also extends to hose-pipes. Humans also appear to have an instinctive fear of small creatures which move swiftly and apparently unpredictably, hence the very common fears of spiders, mice, and similar creatures.

Whereas at one time in our evolution, and still in some parts of the world, an instinctive fear of such creatures as these is life-saving, most of us counteract them with logic. We teach ourselves that, in Britain at any rate, spiders aren't dangerous or lethal. In this way we adjust our instinctive responses to fit in with where and how we live.

Another of these instinctive responses which we humans share with many other four-legged creatures is fear when we sense it in others. A dog which senses fear in its master becomes edgy too. Horses which show fear of an obstacle will become even more afraid if their riders feel fear too.

A good human example of this fear creating fear is with very young babies. A tiny baby can sense when the person holding it is unsure. If this is the case, the baby becomes fearful too and begins to cry.

When each of my own children was newborn my sister visited. At that time she had no children of her own and wasn't accustomed to small babies. She insisted on holding mine. On each occasion, I handed a placid baby to her. Almost as soon as she had it in her arms, the baby would start to cry. I'd take it back and it would stop.

The babies were sensing my sister's inexperience at holding them and were expressing their own concern. When handed to my sister-in-law, however, they didn't mind at all. She was a midwife and well used to tiny babies.

This reaction contributes too, no doubt, to the fact that new parents often experience far greater difficulty with their first child than with subsequent ones. They are more concerned with the first, more afraid of making mistakes and this transmits to the baby who then becomes slightly anxious in return. By the time other children are born, the parents have learned how to cope and their manner is usually far more relaxed, and so too is the child as a result.

Another common situation where this occurs is when a

child is taken to visit the dentist or to hospital in order to have something done about which its mother is anxious. If the mother is anxious, this will be transmitted to the child. Children are programmed by nature to react to the feelings of their mothers, as are other creatures. This again is for survival. The young of any species learn by copying the behaviour of their parents. If the parents show fear in certain circumstances, the young learn to do the same.

Unfortunately, among humans, many parents show anxiety when there's really nothing to be gained by it. In this way they teach their children to become anxious when it's not always to their advantage.

For instance, the parent who's afraid of dental treatment will often transmit this to the child so that the child becomes afraid too. This often also happens when a child is admitted to hospital, especially in an emergency. Although the presence of a parent at its side should reassure the child, the parent becomes distraught. So as to prevent this added distress being conveyed to the child, the parent is removed from the situation and made to wait elsewhere.

Humans all have a basic tendency to be afraid of tiny enclosed spaces – lest they suffocate; heights – lest they fall; unpredictable animals – lest they attack suddenly and harm them; and fear in others – lest the same threat is creeping up on them too. This final example is the one responsible for panic reactions in crowds, for mass hysteria at pop concerts.

Usually all these instinctive fears are put under our conscious, logical control. You may jump when you're working in the garage and something small dashes across the corner of your vision. This is the sentry in your head alerting you to possible danger from small, swift creatures. You turn, heart beating slightly faster, to see what it was, and then breathe a sigh of relief when you see it was only a mouse that you know can do you no harm. The sentry picks up your feelings and switches off the fear reaction.

On the other hand, if you observed that, instead of a small, harmless mouse, the intruder was a large, plague-carrying rat, the fight or flight reaction would begin. (This would also be the reaction of someone afraid of mice, even though they're harmless.

Most of us de-program these instinctive fears. We re-educate the sentries in our heads so that, for instance, we only feel fear of heights if there's a real danger we could actually fall and come to harm in the situation concerned. We only fear enclosed spaces where there's a danger of being trapped or smothered.

Some people, however, have either never re-programmed their sentries in these finer points or, due to a bad experience, have become ultra-sensitive to them, and so go on reacting to them with fear. This is when the fears become phobias. A phobia is simply a fear reaction to a situation which isn't really threatening and to which most people don't react with fear.

SUMMARY

In this chapter I have tried to explain the role of the sentry in your head. I hope it is also clear that, although it reacts without your conscious knowledge, the sentry is still programmed by you, by the way you react to the situations it warns you about. Any new situation, however pleasant, will cause your sentry to put you more on your guard initially. This is normal and you should be aware of this. I shall describe ways of coping with these reactions in Part 2.

LESSON TWO IN UNDERSTANDING

Below I have listed situations which commonly cause people's sentries to assume the 'on guard' position. Consider each one carefully and see if you can understand why, before checking the answers given in Appendix 2.

- Your first day in a new job
- Dressing up to go to a wedding

- Meeting new people
- Embarking upon a course of study at night school if you've never been to night school before
- Giving up work to bring up your baby
- Retirement
- Illness of a member of the family

CHAPTER THREE

Arousal and Personality

If we all have sentries in our heads, which react to new situations warning us to be careful, how is it that some people manage to 'live on the edge'? There are those who seem to have to push themselves into ever more dangerous and different situations in order to feel 'alive', to get their kicks, whilst for others, the mere thought of doing such things sends shudders down the spine.

Just as, normally, we're all born with two arms, two legs, two eyes and so on, so we all have sentries in our heads. But there the similarity ends. Just as we have arms and legs of different lengths and shapes and eyes of different shapes and colours, so too our sentries vary from person to person.

We vary in the amount of newness or danger required to make our sentries wary. Sentries range from the highly alert sentry to the sleepy sentry (see Figure 4). The sleepy sentry, as his name suggests, is the most lethargic. It takes a lot to rouse him. From time to time he may sense danger and may open one eye to assess it, but he won't actually take any action until he's absolutely sure the danger's real.

This is the type of sentry possessed by those people who seem to thrive on danger, excitement and change. Because it takes so much to wake up their sentries in the first place, they are forever seeking, on a regular basis, those situations which the rest of us wouldn't willingly contemplate once in a lifetime! These people often become adventurers, racing

Highly Alert Sentry	Eyes and ears poised
	Constantly looking for danger
	Easily gets anxious
Tea-drinker Sentry	Aware of surroundings but relaxed
	and enjoying himself
Sleepy Sentry	Easily bored
	Tends to 'nod off' or get restless
	if nothing's happening

Figure 4

drivers, Himalayan mountaineers, stunt-men and women, roving war reporters and so on.

At the other extreme is the highly alert sentry. This sentry is 'on guard' almost all the time. It grows suspicious at the least provocation, actively checking out every slight deviation from the usual.

When I explained in the previous chapter how simply playing classical records used to make me slightly anxious, some of you may have wondered what sort of crackpot I was to be so susceptible. I will admit that I used to be very nervy. Staying away from home used to unsettle me. It wasn't that I didn't want to go, but that I couldn't cope with the newness when I got there and used to become edgy and upset. This was interpreted by those looking after me as homesickness.

My sentry used to be of the highly alert kind, wary of even its own shadow. Note that I use the past tense. Where sentries are concerned, although you may be born with one type, there are ways of training it to react differently.

Compare the sentry for a moment with one of your legs. You inherit a certain length of leg and heaviness of bone. Nevertheless, depending on the degree and the way in which you use that leg, you can alter its shape and size a certain amount by developing the potential of the muscles.

You have the same leeway with the sentry in your head. Although it may be of a certain basic type, you are still able to train it a little (I will be telling you how in Part 2). In my own case, I'm now quite content to travel far from home, or to play music with which I'm not familiar without becoming uneasy about it.

Somewhere between the highly alert sentry and the sleepy sentry is the average sentry. This is the one which some people have and others want. It reacts just the right amount. I think of it as the tea drinker. It does its job of watching quite calmly most of the time, mug in hand. It observes carefully but doesn't overreact, neither does it fail to see threat when it's there.

There's a questionnaire at the end of this chapter to help you discover, if you don't already know, which type of sentry you have. Having identified the type, we must consider other factors affected by this, those of arousal and personality.

AROUSAL

We feel increased arousal when our minds work more rapidly, when the sentry becomes wary. We feel reduced arousal when our thoughts slow down and the sentry relaxes. Increased arousal isn't necessarily bad.

A certain degree of arousal is necessary before we can become sufficiently motivated to do anything. Do you remember the example I used in Chapter 1, where the teacher said to the pupil, 'if you're not worried about the exams then you should be!' What the teacher meant wasn't that it was necessary to worry, but that fear of failure might drive the pupil to try harder, might motivate by increasing the pupil's arousal.

Before we consider some everyday examples of apparently incorrect arousal, let us see exactly how arousal and performance relate to one another. Performance in this context refers to how well a person does whatever it is they're trying to do. This may range from doing algebra homework to taking part in the London Marathon. For each person, in each activity, there's a best level of arousal. You're probably well aware, if you think for a moment, of times when you've tried to do something for which you didn't have enough arousal.

Imagine, for instance, that you decide to get up half an hour earlier on Saturday morning so you can tidy the house before going to town. When Saturday morning comes, the bed is warm and comfortable and you remind yourself that since it's Saturday and you don't have to go to work, you don't have to get up. You recall promising yourself you'd do the clearing up before going out today, but you can't really summon up the same enthusiasm for the idea from the cosiness of the bed. The sentry in your head sees nothing in the situation to become active over. Hence you have insufficient arousal for what you intended.

Suppose, however, that you suddenly remembered, as you lay there, that your dreaded Great Aunt Ethel was coming to lunch and that she'd really give you a good ticking off if the place wasn't immaculate. On a rational level you know that Great Aunt Ethel can't do anything about it if the place is untidy when she comes, except make your life a misery by nagging. But when she nags ... The sentry in your head too finds it has uncomfortable memories of Great Aunt Ethel's reprimands. Thus the sentry becomes restless, gradually increasing the arousal until you find that lying in bed has lost its appeal because you're now worrying about the consequences if you don't get a move on.

At the other extreme there are times when too much arousal reduces your ability to do the simplest things. For instance, you can probably dress yourself in very little time under normal circumstances. You probably do it without having to think too much about what you're doing because it's something you do so very often. Things we habitually do normally require a tiny degree of arousal. We're so used to doing them that our sentries know there's no danger whatsoever and remain unmoved. Such things can become so habitual that we can do them automatically, without thinking about them.

One day your alarm clock fails to ring and you wake up to find you've only ten minutes to make it to the bus or you'll be late for work. Suddenly aware of the unpleasant consequences of arriving at work late, the sentry becomes alert and, in doing so, increases your arousal. You now find yourself having to get dressed with a very high level of arousal whereas the task normally requires virtually none. This increased arousal makes you all fingers and thumbs. The movements that usually come naturally are suddenly difficult and you tie yourself up in all sorts of knots . . . This is the result of arousal that's too high for the situation concerned.

Thus, it might be argued that there's a best level of arousal for every task. This best level varies from person to person, from task to task, and even from day to day. You might need a higher level of arousal to do the same task one day than you do on another. We all have to learn to recognize when we've reached our own best level of arousal for whatever we're doing. Not only recognize when we've reached it, but be able to keep it there.

The first part is fairly easy in that most of us know when we're either too aroused or not aroused enough. The difficulties arise when we try to keep the arousal at the correct level. Very public demonstrations of such difficulties occur frequently in sport.

The Role of Arousal in Sport

Many of the problems with drug-taking in sport are based on attempts to control arousal levels.

At one end of the scale we hear of track athletes taking stimulants. These are drugs which increase the arousal level when the athlete feels insufficiently motivated.

As we saw with Trog and the mammoth in Chapter 1, increased arousal prepares the body for physical activity, fight or flight. It is obvious, then, why increased arousal is helpful, or even necessary, to an athlete. Perhaps you or I, taking part in school sports day, may have been sufficiently aroused by the occasion itself and the fact that friends and relations had come to watch, to run as fast as we could. The occasion didn't arise often enough for us to get used to it.

The situation is sometimes different for highly successful

athletes who have taken part in hundreds of competitions before, and have competed against the same participants many times. Sometimes, for them, the occasion alone and the challenge of the other competitors may be insufficient to arouse them enough.

Well-trained athletes are generally able to find a way to 'psych themselves up' and increase their arousal. A professional footballer I heard of used to become so aroused before a match that he'd be physically sick before going onto the pitch. Unfortunately some have been driven to taking illegal stimulants in order to enhance their own arousal and so help their performance.

It would probably be better if those who participated in competitive athletics had sentries who were fairly easily aroused – more like the highly alert sentry than the sleepy one. This is usually the case with racehorses, for instance. These horses are frequently what's termed 'highly strung' – which is the popular way of saying 'has a highly alert sentry'. This trait is largely, if not totally, inherited since they are bred from other successful racehorses. Yet it's what helps to make them race well.

At the other end of the scale there are sports in which high arousal is a disadvantage. Sports where a competitor requires a steady hand and eye, a slowed heart-rate, a calculating mind. Sports where the optimum level of arousal for the best performance is low, such as snooker or darts. These are the sports where the drug-taking problem isn't concerned with stimulants but with tranquillizers. The most commonly reported of these in this context are the beta blockers.

Beta blockers are used in heart complaints to maintain the rhythm. But because, when we become anxious, our heart rate increases, beta blockers have been used to treat anxiety disorders as well. In sports such as shooting, darts, and snooker, for example, it is obvious that beta blockers could be beneficial to a competitor whose arousal was too high. Just as we become all fingers and thumbs if forced to dress in a hurry, so too much arousal in sports such as these can impair performance.

Often, when watching snooker matches, I've seen the player who isn't expected to win playing some of his best snooker. This player takes the lead because he isn't expecting to do well anyhow and is relaxing and just enjoying the game. Suddenly finding himself in the lead, however, he wonders what he's doing there. The sentry in his head becomes alert because this isn't a situation it's used to. The arousal increases. Gradually this player misses shots, makes mistakes, each failure making him more uncomfortable, keeping his sentry alert. Finally his opponent wins the match.

Some snooker players, it seems, have learnt well how to keep their sentries under control in these situations. Those who go to pieces when they begin to do well are those who haven't.

There are, of course, many variations on this theme, such as those who begin by doing badly and worry over it. This leads to even worse mistakes as the worry increases the arousal above the best level. Sentry management is something which would be advantageous to all sports people to learn as well as for the rest of us. As I've already said, you *can* train the sentry you're born with so that it responds in ways more appropriate to the life you lead.

PERSONALITY

In humans, certain personality traits tend to be associated with those whose sentries are highly alert. As with racehorses, people with highly alert sentries are often described as being 'highly strung'. This generally means that they react to situations with greater emotion than the average person – they become more upset over misfortunes, more easily angered, easily afraid. This doesn't have to be the case, however. A person with a highly alert sentry can learn to change. Easily aroused people also tend to be obsessional in various ways. I shall explain more about obsessive behaviours and the reasons for them in the next chapter.

Constant high levels of anxiety-type arousal can lead to

various stress-induced illnesses such as heart attacks. It is not surprising to find that a certain type of personality has been shown to be common amongst people who have these stress-induced diseases. This is known as a Type A personality.

The Type A person is often said to be a high achiever, always trying to be the best. Someone who likes things to be done precisely how and when they should be, and who worries if they aren't. Type A people have often been described as workaholics who can't relax.

In many respects I would agree with all these things except that we should look beneath the surface and ask ourselves why they behave like this. Why the striving for perfection and the constant race against time?

The answer lies in a sentry who becomes wary and who is then kept in this wary state. The Type A person is one whose sentry is wide awake and aroused and who is rarely given permission to 'stand at ease' because the owner doesn't know how.

Other people find constant high arousal such as this can be exhilarating. There are those who claim to thrive on stress. Often it happens in someone whose sentry has been the staid tea-drinker variety. Someone whose life has chugged along but has lacked extra sparkle. All at once, somehow, the sentry becomes highly alert due to high pressures of work or something similar. The person finds this quite thrilling and seeks more and more of this high arousal. Unfortunately, because it can be exhilarating, the person becomes almost addicted to it and keeps it going. The body, however, isn't made to tolerate this and eventually burns itself out in stress.

Again, it is possible to be a high-achiever without endangering yourself. It all comes down to training your sentry. One final point about training your sentry lies in its readiness to learn and how this varies from person to person.

Shakespeare was very perceptive when he wrote in *Julius Caesar*: 'The evil that men do lives after them, the good is oft interred with their bones . . .'

Why do we remember the bad things rather than the

good? Because nature made us that way. When something bad happens to us, nature wants to ensure that we aren't likely to put ourselves in such a position again because it could threaten our survival. Thus, our sentries react very quickly when they become aware of anything which had an unpleasant outcome on a previous occasion. They remind us of the consequences and we become anxious or afraid and try to get out of the situation.

Introverts and Extroverts

It has been found that people who are introverts tend to avoid potentially unpleasant situations even more vehemently than extroverts. What are introverts and extroverts?

Very generally, introverts are regarded as those people who prefer their own company, who don't need the company of other people a great deal in order to feel content. Extroverts, on the other hand, are those who enjoy mixing with others. They need other people around them in order to feel alive.

It is thought that introverts have more highly alert sentries than extroverts. Their preference for avoiding social gatherings is a way of avoiding arousal, which is relatively easily increased once they mix with others and venture outside their usual way of life. Whereas extroverts have far less highly alert sentries and so can put up with more before becoming mildly aroused.

For instance, suppose Trog, instead of having to run away from the mammoth, jumps into the water and joins the cave-woman. He hasn't played around in water like this before and his sentry becomes wary because something new and different is going on. Trog, however, decides he's enjoying this new experience. This is relayed to his sentry, who relaxes. Trog thus feels excitement rather than anxiety.

Your sentry arouses you because something different is happening. You then label what you're feeling about it as anxiety or excitement and your sentry reacts accordingly. In the case of anxiety it makes you watchful of danger, distracting you from everything else, tensing your muscles for action. If, however, you tell your sentry the arousal is excitement, the sentry goes back to guarding and allows you to relax, thus enjoying the arousal (see Figure 5, p.42).

It has been suggested that perhaps extroverts are more inclined to tell their sentries that the high arousal they feel is excitement rather than anxiety or fear. The introvert, disliking high arousal, is more likely to label it anxiety and so trains the sentry to react accordingly. Hence, whereas the extrovert sees a party as exciting, the introvert has learned to react to it with anxiety and to avoid it if possible.

SUMMARY

In this chapter we have looked at what arousal is and how it relates to our personalities.

We have seen too how some people are easily aroused and so tend not to seek out settings and situations which may increase this too much or too rapidly. Other people are very slow to become aroused and seem to look for thrills and danger. This is because they need this greater degree of stimulation in order to feel excited.

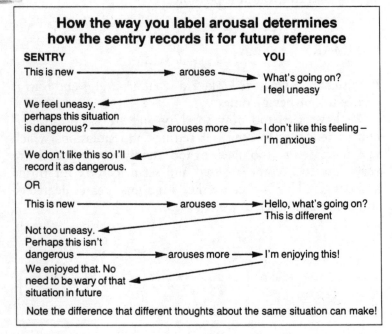

How the way you label arousal determines how the sentry records it for future reference

SENTRY   YOU

This is new ──────────▶ arouses ──────▶ What's going on?
                                                  I feel uneasy

We feel uneasy. ◀──
perhaps this situation
is dangerous? ──────────▶ arouses more ──────▶ I don't like this feeling –
                                                  I'm anxious

We don't like this so I'll ◀──
record it as dangerous.

OR

This is new ──────────▶ arouses ──────▶ Hello, what's going on?
                                                  This is different

Not too uneasy. ◀──
Perhaps this isn't
dangerous ──────────▶ arouses more ──────▶ I'm enjoying this!

We enjoyed that. No
need to be wary of that ◀──
situation in future

Note the difference that different thoughts about the same situation can make!

Figure 5

LESSON THREE IN UNDERSTANDING

This questionnaire is to help you identify the type of sentry you have and certain relevant personality traits.

1. Tick any of the following situations which would provoke any *unpleasant* high arousal in you beforehand:
    Taking an important exam
    Going to a formal dinner
    Competing in a sporting event
    Making a speech
    Visiting the dentist
    Score 1 point for each one ticked =

2. Tick any of the following which would provoke any *unpleasant* high arousal in you as they happen:
    Being stuck in a traffic jam when you're going to be late
    Having an injection
    Feeling unwell
    Being at a social gathering
    Being reprimanded by someone in authority
    Cooking a meal for guests
    Score 1 point for each one ticked =

3. Do you enjoy your work best when you're able to chat to colleagues as you work on joint projects or when you work on things alone? Circle your answer and score accordingly.

1	2	3	4	5
always with others	usually with others	bit of both	usually alone	always alone

4. When you attend a social function, party, etc. do you prefer the other guests to be strangers at first so you're able to get to know them? Or do you prefer it if the other guests are people you already know well? Circle your answer and score accordingly.

1	2	3	4	5
all	mostly	half	mostly	all
strangers	strangers	& half	familiar	familiar

5. How do you feel about people who drop in unexpectedly? Circle your answer and score accordingly.

1	2	3	4	5
love it	usually	sometimes	prefer	hate it
	love it	OK	they	
			don't	

6. If your partner came home Friday night and said that, as a surprise, you were both off for a weekend break abroad, which reaction would be most typical of you? Circle your answer and score accordingly.

5	4	3	2	1
panic-stricken and not wanting to go	you wish you'd been warned and are apprehensive	you'd like to go but you have commitments	pleased once the idea's sunk in	really excited and can't wait

7. Which of the following thoughts would be most typical of you on being told that your garden shed had been broken into?

a) Oh dear! This shouldn't have happened. Nothing like this has ever happened in our neighbourhood before.

b) There's no point worrying, it's happened. I'd better go and see what the damage is so I can get onto the insurance company and get things sorted out as soon as possible.

c) I wonder what I should do now? I'd better ring my husband/wife/mother/father/friend and ask them.

   Score 1 point for b)
       2 points for c)
       3 points for a)

Add up your total score. How did you do?

Less than 10 : You're either an extrovert with a sleepy sentry or you've already learned to cope with unpleasant high arousal and you don't need this book at all.

11 – 20 : You seem to cope fairly well. Your sentry doesn't appear to over-react – probably the tea-drinker type. You could enhance your enjoyment of life by attempting to make your reactions a little more like those which earn lower scores than yours. After all, if you can't change something, let it go and get on with life as it is now.

21 – 34 : Your sentry seems to be of the highly alert kind. The nearer your score is to the maximum of 34, the more you react with unpleasant high arousal. This book is for you. Hopefully, given time and practice, your score will reduce considerably.

CHAPTER FOUR

Control

What is the one fear which is shared by more people than any other? I'll give you some clues ... It's not something that most people realize they're afraid of until it confronts them. It's not one of the commonly mentioned fears such as spiders, heights, blood and so on. Do you know yet?

Look at the title of this chapter for another clue ... got it? Yes, the fear more of us have than any other is the fear of *Losing control*!

Now, losing control means different things to different people. Some fear losing control of their lives, their finances, their home life, their children. Other people fear losing control of their thoughts or their bodies. Some people fear losing control of all of these.

Of course, in order to fear losing control of something, you must think that you have control of it in the first place. Children, for example, never having yet had control of their day-to-day lives, don't fear losing this control at all. As the old saying goes, what you never had you don't miss. Most children, however, whilst accepting the control of adults whilst they're small, would soon rebel in their teens if this control wasn't gradually handed to them. With maturity comes the desire to run our own lives.

Before we examine control further, let me demonstrate how fear of losing control in one area of my life used to affect me.

When I married my husband he already had three children, aged from 6 to 11, living with him. It wasn't easy being a fair and reasonable stepmother, especially for me, as I was the sort of person who liked to run the home my way. I wasn't able to put up easily with others interfering with my plans and arrangements.

Added to this was the complication that, whereas most of us feel we can yell at our own children knowing they won't take serious offence, stepchildren are different. If they're reprimanded for the slightest thing, they take it personally and tend to think you don't love them any more. Thus I used to have to walk a tightrope in order to maintain the control I thought I needed without causing unnecessary upsets.

From time to time the eldest stepchild would try to test me by provoking me and questioning the need for my rules. Inevitably after such confrontations I'd have a particular dream. In this dream my stepson would be deliberately doing all those things which in real life I'd have hated him to do. He'd bring hoards of friends into the house and raid the freezer. Then they'd cook huge feasts and leave the kitchen in chaos.

As this was going on in my dream, I'd be watching, screaming and shouting at them all to leave – but no sound ever came out of my mouth! I'd be completely powerless – total loss of control. Afterwards I'd wake up sweaty and shaken, but relieved to find it was only a dream. The result was, however, that for a time I'd become even more restrictive. This wasn't done consciously. In retrospect I can see that it was a form of compensation. I was making doubly sure that the dream never had the chance to happen for real.

What is control? Control is having things happen as and when you expect they will. The most predictable events in life are those that have become routine. When something happens at a regular time and to a regular pattern, that is classed in your head as usual, as routine.

If you think back for a moment to Chapter 3, what was it

that aroused the sentry least? It was when the sentry knew what to expect, when it knew from experience that a situation wasn't likely to be dangerous or frightening. This is what routine situations are – non-arousing to the sentry.

CONTROL AND PREDICTABILITY

When we want better to understand our most basic ways of reacting, the answers can often be found in the behaviour of babies and toddlers. To a great extent, very small children still react most naturally to life as they've not had the time yet to readjust their reactions according to their experiences. Babies and small children love routine and react badly to the loss of it. Ask any parent of a young baby what happens when that baby's routine is seriously disrupted.

Now, just as there are some adults with sleepy sentries, who can take no end of disruption and upheaval before they become alarmed, so too there are some very placid babies who also appear to have sleepy sentries. These babies are the ones who seem to be able to take all kinds of unusual situations in their stride, some who even seem to thrive on it! Some of you may have observed that relatively rare phenomenon of the baby who not only doesn't cry at its christening, but who actually smiles at the vicar! Such babies are the exception. Most have sentries which are aroused by the strange place, the strange clothes, the strange faces, and, above all, having strange things done to them, with the result that the baby shows its disapproval in no uncertain terms.

I still recall vividly the day my husband and I took our baby son to visit his grandparents at their home for the first time. We'd travelled a couple of hundred miles by car and arrived late at night. The baby slept in his cot in the car, as he often did.

We unloaded the car at our destination, the baby was hugged and fussed over for a while, then we all prepared to go to bed. The baby, however, wasn't willing. We settled him in his cot in the bedroom, but he screamed. I picked him up, quietened him, put him back down, and he screamed again. This went on for over an hour and we were beginning to worry in case the neighbours were being kept awake as well. It was by this time about two in the morning. I was worn out, my husband was worn out, his parents were exhausted, but the baby seemed ready to continue for hours (no doubt on account of the sleep he'd had on the journey there).

In desperation we decided to put him in the car, in his cot, and drive around until he fell asleep. We bundled everything out again into the cold night and set off. Within some five minutes of leaving the bungalow, our son was sleeping peacefully.

Not wanting to seem too eager, however, we drove around for a further half hour, just to make sure he was really asleep, then headed back. We parked the car and unloaded the cot as quietly as we could. We crept back into the house, placed the cot in the bedroom and turned to get ready for bed ourselves. Just as we turned out the light, he started again! (Refreshed by his sleep in the car no doubt!) Finally my mother-in-law called the doctor, who administered the knock-out drops to the baby, and we all finally had a good night's sleep.

By the following night, however, our son had become accustomed to the new surroundings and went to sleep like an angel.

Repetition is another form of routine which is loved by small children. Adults are often amazed that a child will want to eat the same foods day after day. They may try to convince the child that it might be good to try something different, but often the child doesn't want to know. Children also like the same stories read to them time and again, in preference to new ones. They like their favourite TV programmes to be screened at the same time each day.

All these routines, same stories, same foods, same environments, are un-arousing to the sentry. As such, they do not arouse the person unduly. Why is it that small children seem to have a greater need for this sameness than adults? After all, even the most anxiety-prone adult tends to like some variation in foods, in entertainment.

My theory is that it's because small children have so much to learn about the world they're living in that each ordinary day brings dozens of new sensations to them. They hear new words, see new textures and colours, hear new sounds. All this newness is potentially arousing to the sentry. Thus, so that the sentry's arousal is kept to an enjoyable level, as much of the child's life as possible is controlled by predictability – by eating familiar foods, hearing familiar stories, living according to a familiar routine.

As I mentioned above, some babies, like some adults, appear to have sleepy sentries and to be able to encounter new and different experiences without becoming as uncomfortably aroused as most of us. Such people seem to avoid routines and predictability in their lives as if they need the extra kick that unpredictability gives them in order to feel they're living.

In contrast are those people whose sentries are easily aroused. Such people seem to be even more keen than most to live according to routines. The more threatened and anxious they feel, the more routines they introduce into their lives, and the more restrictive they become.

Think back to the example I gave earlier in this chapter of my relationship with my stepchildren. Because I tended to be afraid of losing control, I used to be over-restrictive. The more threatened I felt, the more restrictive I became.

Such restrictions in an anxious person's life don't always relate directly to what they're afraid of losing control of. For instance, at this time in my life I also became very obsessional about the housework. In other words, my general state of insecurity and threatened loss of control caused me to try and calm my sentry by introducing as much predictability into my daily life as I could, and so reduce my general level of unpleasant arousal (anxiety). I used to have to clean a particular room on a particular day each week. I was unable to bear to leave it for once, I was too afraid all the work would get out of hand.

So, as you see, obsessions, although they bring routines and predictability into the person's life, don't also bring reduced anxiety. The person then becomes ruled by the obsessions, as I was with my housework. They become afraid of not fulfilling them, thus the obsessions no longer serve to keep the sentry un-aroused by making life routine. Instead, the obsessions themselves arouse anxiety because the person fears not fulfilling them. Thus, by definition, obsessional people are often also anxiety-prone people.

Obsessions don't increase a person's sense of control, they reduce it. This reduced sense of control often brings about an increase in the obsessions in a misguided attempt to introduce predictability and, with it, greater control. *But* control entails more than just predictability. Control is predictability plus something else.

CONTROL AND UNDERSTANDING

A few years ago a lady called Linda was sent to me by her GP. Linda had recently given up her job and was now at home with a new baby to care for. She explained that before the baby had been born she'd done both a full-time job and run the home without difficulty. She used to have routines for doing the weekly shop and the washing and so on, and had generally felt relaxed and happy. Since being at home with the baby, however, all that had changed.

Now she said that she constantly felt anxious and ill-at-ease. She said she had plenty of free time, something she'd always yearned for more of when she'd been at work, but she couldn't enjoy it. Her constant sense of unease had slowly increased such that she was beginning to feel panicky both when she went anywhere or stayed at home.

Linda's increased anxiety, it transpired, was the result of having lost her routines. The arrival of the new baby and the giving up of her job had changed drastically the pattern of Linda's life. Although she wasn't threatened by any serious situation, her sentry was reacting to the change and making her uneasy. Since she also had plenty of free time, something she wasn't accustomed to, she hadn't felt the need to organize her time as she'd had to do before.

The result of all this change and new freedom was that Linda's life had lost any pattern. Linda, however, hadn't recognized this. As far as she was concerned, she now had all this free time to enjoy her baby and yet she felt uneasy. She became more and more anxious about the way she felt. This in turn kept her sentry aroused too.

We will learn in Chapter 8 exactly how Linda overcame her problem. For now it is sufficient that her story shows us the second important aspect of control – that of understanding. Control isn't true control unless we understand how and why it's there. Had Linda realized why she'd been feeling uneasy at the changes in her life, she could have talked herself round and overcome the problem herself.

Resistance to Understanding

Those of us who work in the field of mental health frequently come up against the problem of finding acceptable reasons for the way we are. Even in our so-called enlightened society there are those people who think that any help received to overcome an illness or minor problem in the mind is less socially acceptable than receiving help to cure a problem of the body.

If you break your leg you don't try and hide the fact that you've been to hospital to have it put in plaster. Everyone knows that a broken leg has to be set by doctors. Everyone is also able to see actual evidence of the injury on the X-ray.

If, however, you have an anxiety problem, or a phase of depression, we only have your word for how you feel. If you seek professional help, you don't broadcast the fact in case other people see it as a weakness or as making a fuss about nothing. Thus, very often we find that some people, even when they've sought help for a psychological or even a psychiatric problem, still try to believe it's physical in origin. One patient of mine, we'll call him John, provided a wonderful example of this.

John was referred to me because he suffered with back

aches which became worse when he experienced problems at work. At first John insisted that there was some real injury to his back following a sports accident some months earlier. Hospital investigations had so far proved negative. Beside the possible physical injury, moreover, John had real problems with his job. His was the classic case of someone who'd been doing really well in the job for which he'd been trained, and was content and enjoying himself. Because he was so good at his job, however, his bosses decided he should be promoted. He was promoted from a practical job to a desk job. He was no longer 'one of the boys' going out, fixing things. Now he was management.

At first he didn't mind too much. The increase in pay compensated for the loss of the companionship of his workmates. Gradually, however, John grew frustrated with the new job. He found himself working for a very unreasonable superior who never let him complete a piece of work before dragging him off to begin the next. Slowly he lost his sense of contentment. He began to feel hunted and dissatisfied at work. He could no longer predict what he'd have to do each day or each week. He was unable to complete a list of jobs well done. He was constantly at the mercy of the unpredictable whims of his boss.

As his sense of control at work lessened, so John's back aches and anxiety increased. Treatment entailed helping John to understand what was happening at work so he could devise routines based on a different set of expectations from those he'd used in his previous job. John, however, was unable to accept deep down that the roots of his problem were psychological rather than caused by his back injury.

This was finally made clear when one day he asked in desperation for 'some other type of pill' to ease the pain. His GP was willing to prescribe but John was unwilling to take any form of pain killer that might be addictive, and in the end there was nothing which was both non-addictive yet sufficiently strong to ease his pain. In desperation John was forced to admit to himself that perhaps his back ache was at least partly psychological. From that moment on he tried harder with his relaxation and hypnosis tapes as a way of overcoming the tension that caused the pain.

The outcome of John's case a few months later was truly remarkable. It's sufficient to point out that it wasn't until John finally realized that there weren't any drugs that were acceptable to him that he finally believed his problem to be psychological and therefore curable by psychological means. This was the turning point in his treatment.

Another patient, Angela, had a similar experience. She had severe attacks of anxiety. She was taught psychological ways of coping but she never really put these into practice. At the back of her mind she believed that the true cause of her attacks was a brain tumour. Finally, one day when I told her that I wasn't going to see her again because my treatment was obviously doing no good, she was forced to face up to the situation. She began to really believe that her anxiety was psychologically caused and to do as she'd been taught to alleviate it. From that day on she began to improve.

Time and again I know that although a patient says they understand their symptoms, they really believe that there's a pill somewhere that will cure them. Not until they finally accept this false assumption for what it is and start to take matters into their own hands, do they begin to get better.

In order to overcome illness, an element of control needs to be accepted by the patient. In psychological problems, that control has to be accepted almost totally. In physical illness it can be partially given to the doctor, but it helps if the patient also believes that they too can help make themselves better. It is now believed that cancer patients have a better survival rate if they believe that they too have a part to play in making themselves better rather than feeling they're at the total mercy of the doctors.

People tend to think that any illness they have must surely be physically caused for several reasons. One is because, as we've seen, physical illness is more acceptable to other people. No blame is attached to it – it's 'not your fault'.

A second reason is that if you have a physical illness, it's up to doctors to cure you. There's little you can do for yourself – the responsibility is theirs.

A third reason is that most of us can understand why we feel ill if there's a physical cause. We can see the evidence of test results and so on. There is no evidence that's available for study in the case of psychological illness. Thus it's harder to accept.

So, control involves both predictability and understanding. Before we accept control of something we have to understand it. Angela and John were unable to exert control over their psychological problems and begin to overcome them until they stopped believing the problems had primarily physical causes.

SINGLE WOMEN, MARRIED MEN

Control means different things to different people. For instance, some people enjoy being tidy and feel threatened, their sentries aroused, if forced to live with someone who is untidy. To other people tidiness is unimportant, they're quite content to be unable to find anything without a search.

There is an interesting statistic that says psychological problems based on anxiety – that is, stress, nervous break-downs, and so on – occur in more single men than married men, but in more married women than single women. Thus, if you want peace of mind and you're a man, you should marry: if you're a woman, however, you'd be better off staying single. These statistics make sense if we look at them in terms of control.

Many's the time in recent years I've read an interview with a successful woman in a magazine where she's been quoted as saying she wished she had a wife to cope with the household while she concentrated on her career. This, of course, is what married men have traditionally had for decades – a wife at home to organize their lives for them, to keep their homes under control. They have been able to enjoy having a family, a home, their laundry and meals attended to, leaving them with more time and energy to devote to their jobs.

The single man, on the other hand, has not only to work, but also care for his laundry, shopping and so on. All this without the emotional closeness of a family. He has far more things to try to gain control of at once.

But, you say, the single woman is surely in the same position? To some extent, yes. On the other hand, for centuries little girls have been raised with a knowledge of how to do basic household chores and, most importantly, with the expectation that one day they will have to do it for themselves. It's like cleaning their teeth or washing their hair. In most, the ability to look after themselves in this way is so routine as to be totally un-arousing to their sentries. Although enlightened parents are now raising their sons to be as domestically capable as their daughters, there are whole generations of men who were raised by parents whose expectations of life were very different.

When I was a child, married women devoted themselves to caring for their families first and foremost. They saw to the needs of their sons until they married, when their wives took over the task. Social changes of various kinds have now left many of these sons to cope on their own. Although many are willing to try, the ability to do so is not as naturally acceptable to them as it was to their sisters and it imposes additional arousal on their sentries, making them more vulnerable than married men to anxiety symptoms.

Married women are vulnerable because they are expected to cope with so many aspects of life which are not totally under their control. They are expected to be all things to their families, yet many also have careers of their own. The way their attention has to be spread in so many directions means that perhaps they never really feel in control of any of it, but swept along from day to day at the mercy of whatever crops up.

These are, of course, gross generalizations. We all know individuals who aren't affected in this way. Not every vulnerable person succumbs to anxiety disorders. Of those that do, the reasons may lie in the outlines given above. Society has changed so very much in the last twenty years in the expectations put upon men and women that we must be careful not to take things at face value. If someone is unable to cope, it isn't just a question of whether they have the ability to cope, but also of whether they ever expected to have to cope.

Having to muddle your way through something you aren't mentally prepared for is just as arousing to the sentry as being in a strange place. If you suddenly find yourself having to cope with such unexpected demands at a time when you're also emotionally upset, such as after a bereavement or divorce, then you're doubly vulnerable.

Evidence[3] is also now being published to show that our resistance to infections of various sorts, be it colds, flu, or whatever, is lowered if we're suffering from stress or worry. My Victorian grandmother always maintained that if you had enough to do you didn't have time to be ill. A more likely explanation in the light of present findings is that people who have something to get on with that they enjoy keep their immune systems healthy and don't therefore fall victims to the bugs that afflict others, especially those who are either unhappy with their lot, or who always look on the black side.

It is important that we consider life, not only as it is but also as it will be, when raising today's children so that they can cope with tomorrow better than the adults of today.

Finally, let us look back at the definitions I gave at the end of Chapter 1 in the light of control and predictability (or expectation).

We can leave aside fear and anxiety, as we're defining them here, because these are normal responses which have no untoward consequences if correctly handled at the time. It is the other three variations on the natural responses of fear and anxiety – those of stress, worry and guilt – to which we will direct our attention.

Stress was defined as 'endless anxiety or worry to which the mind and body keep reacting because the cause is unresolved'. A constant but unsuccessful striving to gain control of whatever is arousing the sentry.

John's stress at work after his promotion was caused by his boss's unpredictable demands and the fact that John was unable to complete one job at a time to his own satisfaction. This resulted in an almost constant feeling of unease, an aroused sentry because John's own expectations of himself, of jobs well done to his own standards, was never met. Predictability was never achieved, so the sentry didn't relax. Since his sentry was almost constantly aroused somewhat anyway, it took only a slight added trigger to make John really anxious.

Such an unending sense of unease and dissatisfaction, which then makes the person very vulnerable to even slight upsets, is typical of stress.

Worry, on the other hand, is anxiety about something over which the person can't exert any influence. Mary's worry over her daughter's marriage is an instance of this. In short, worry is an attempt to control something over which you have no control whatsoever.

Guilt is a variation of worry. This time, however, it is worry over something which has passed. Guilt is a form of obsessionality. It is the constant thinking over of something you did which you didn't do the way you think you should have. You constantly think about it almost as if, by rethinking it, you can change what happened. This attempt at control of what's passed is obviously doomed to failure. Depending on how often the thoughts occur, a reaction similar to stress results.

In Part Two we will, of course, look at ways to escape from these apparently impossible situations where the mind wants to control the uncontrollable. It is not until we can break free of this vicious circle that we are able to relieve our sentries and relax.

SUMMARY

This chapter has tried to show how, by trying to be in control, most people are doing exactly the opposite. Control really boils down to what you *think* rather than what you *do* and whether you can exert influence over others.

Whatever your own interpretation of control, self confidence and contentment result from feeling you're in control of what you think you should be. By definition, if you're not content then either you have to obtain greater control *or* you have to stop trying to be in control of things which you have no hope of controlling. It is the latter which is often the solution.

LESSON FOUR IN UNDERSTANDING

1. List all the things that you are worrying about at the moment or which you have worried about recently.
2. Go through this list item by item and note exactly what *you* can do about each one – if anything. It is important that you only write what you personally can do, not what you want to try to make others do.

Keep this list to refer to later in Chapter 8.

CHAPTER FIVE

Memory Windows

Christmas has always been a special time of year to me. At school I developed the habit of making cards and gift tags for the family and close friends. I still do this as often as I can, time and other commitments permitting.

A few years ago, at around Christmas time, I happened to be treating a young lady who worked as a graphic artist. One particular day, she told me about her design for cards for that year and how she would silk screen print them.

Now, although I always like to make cards at Christmas, I've always had to choose my designs carefully because I can't draw everything. In fact, apart from holly, Christmas trees, and candles, I can't draw much! I was telling this to Paula, bemoaning the fact that I couldn't draw robins.

'They never look real,' I said, picking up a pencil and demonstrating. 'They always look like this!'

In fairness she did try not to laugh. Then she sat back and looked at me. 'You don't draw what you see,' she said simply.

I looked at my robin and I saw what she meant. My mind had said to me, 'A robin has a head, a body, wings, two spindly legs, and a short tail.' That was what I'd drawn.

Had I, however, taken the trouble to really 'see' a robin, I'd have noticed that its head isn't distinguishable from its body, the two blend together as one.

From that one simple guiding statement, Paula inadvertently gave me far more than a drawing lesson. She gave me an insight that I would be able to translate into psychological terms and use in therapy. Which I have done ever since, with great success. I will explain this further later on, but first I want to explain how and why it is that we don't always 'see' what's really there.

Having noted already that our sentries are calmed by predictability and routine, we need to be aware of the extent of this. In actual fact, our brains are designed so as to search for predictability and patterns. Whenever we encounter anything new, our sentry immediately scans its banks of accumulated knowledge until it finds something as similar as it can to the new information. This past information then forms the pane of glass which is put into our memory window. Through this window we then 'see' the present.

Depending on the nature of the pane of glass from memory, our experience of the present situation is distorted by varying degrees. Having selected what it considers to be a relevant window, and provided this window isn't associated with unpleasant feelings, the sentry will then relax again and let you get on with it. If, however, the pane of glass selected does conjure unpleasant feelings, the sentry will stay alert and try to divert you away from the danger by evoking the fear or anxiety response.

Let us take some examples, beginning with one involving neutral feelings. Suppose your friend shows you a new coat she's just bought. You exclaim, 'That's very smart. What an unusual colour!' As your eyes take in the unusual colour, your brain is comparing it to all the colours it has names for in order to name this one.

If you're a visually uncreative person with little ability to recall different shades of colour, you may simply categorize this new coat as 'green'. If, on the other hand, you have a wide knowledge of different shades and hues, you may be able to describe this colour far more precisely as, perhaps, ripe Granny Smith, pale peppermint, avocado, and so on. Whatever your brain finds to compare this new colour with, it will remember it that way. The further out your first labelling was, the harder you'll find it to memorize the colour exactly. The more accurate the first memorized match, the more likely it is you'll be able to go out and buy a pair of gloves the same colour as your friend's coat from memory.

EVENTS AND MEMORY WINDOWS

The same process applies to events. This is, in part, how phobias develop. The memory windows your sentry puts in place contain feelings as well as the perceptions of your senses.

Let us suppose that you've only been to one funeral in your life and you suddenly find yourself faced with having to attend another. As you anticipate the event, your sentry will search for an appropriate memory window for you. In all probability it will choose the one of the other funeral you attended.

Once the memory window is in place, you'll tend to anticipate that this funeral will be like the last, unless you deliberately make yourself think otherwise. Thus, if the first was on a cold day, you'll possibly associate feeling cold with funerals and tend to dress more warmly than you otherwise might.

Taking the experience a step further, if your memory window contains feelings that you found unpleasant, if, for instance, you felt faint during the service, you may begin to view the prospect with a certain amount of dread. Under these circumstances the sentry remains on alert. It may then be that, because of your aroused state, you become easily upset at this funeral too and suffer unpleasant experiences again. In all probability you would then tend to avoid future funerals. This is how some phobias begin to develop.

Strangely, pleasant feelings in a memory window can also create problems. Suppose you were promised a ride in your friend's new Rolls Royce. You jump at the chance. Your sentry provides the memory window of the time when you won a prize trip to the races and part of the prize was that you rode in a Rolls Royce.

At this point, because your arousal is interpreted by you as pleasant rather than unpleasant, your sentry relaxes and you're able to enjoy the arousal. You become excited and expect great things of your ride because that's how it was before. The ride, however, although pleasant, is merely a ride and doesn't live up to your expectations. Perhaps then you feel let down. This negative experience is then attached to the particular memory window by your sentry, replacing the old associations. Now, in future when you're offered a ride in a Rolls Royce and the sentry brings out the appropriate memory window, it will bear the slightly tainted emotion you've just experienced and so you tend to see your next experience in that light.

The reverse can also happen, of course. You may have been provided with a very dull and uninteresting memory window through which to view your new experience, but the experience itself may be so fantastic that it results in the memory window changing in a positive direction. It is this type of change that often happens, for example, when we fall in love.

You've heard people talk of 'seeing the world through rose-coloured glasses'? Well, when you're in love, in those first passionate days or weeks when everything seems wonderful, you're subtly changing all the memory windows you're using so that they have good feelings associated with them. All your experiences are becoming slightly rose-tinted. I've known people who were experiencing anxieties and phobias of various types overcome them completely at times such as these. The rose-tinted memory window tends to override any other and bring a sense of warmth and well-being to everything you do.

There is a similar occurrence with the 'blue' memory window, in that it tends to colour all your experiences with its blue tinge of sadness or unhappiness. If you're deeply upset about something, this tends to affect everything you feel and do, making you sad and giving you sad memories.

Both the rose and the blue tints tend to fade with time.

Because of the way our sentry constantly seeks to compare any new experience with a stored memory we are, in effect, seeing the world via our memories, rather than as it really is. This tendency can have obvious unfortunate repercussions in someone who has had a great many unpleasant memories.

Because our sentries put these memory windows in place without our being conscious of them, they can hamper us when we need to see things as they really are, as with me and the robin. Again, small children's perceptions of the world are often refreshing because they are less hampered by these stored comparisons.

Suppose, just down the road from you, is a white house. One day you take your three-year-old niece for a walk past the house at sunset. The next day she decides to draw a picture of that house. When the picture's finished, you see that she's coloured the walls pink. 'That house was white,' you say. The child remains adamant that the house was pink. Finally you realize that it was sunset when you saw the house. With the glow of the setting sun on its walls, the house did indeed look pink.

To you it was basically still a white house. Although your eyes picked up the colour pink, your brain made adjustments for the fact that it was sunset and you may not even have noticed that the house appeared pink. The child, however, wasn't aware of the effects of the sunset and saw the house as it actually was – as pink!

Such instances happen constantly and we're often unaware of them. We tend to see the world via our 'memory windows', our recorded interpretations of what our eyes, noses and ears perceive – not as our senses actually pick things up. Later in the book I shall discuss ways you can regain the power of your senses when it's to your advantage to do so.

The importance of this for control is that successful control rests upon being able to switch to seeing things as they really are when you need to.

SUMMARY

This chapter has tried to show that a great deal of the time we don't react to reality at all, but to what we *think* is reality. Control relies on our being able to go back to seeing life through the eyes of a child.

LESSON FIVE IN UNDERSTANDING

Spend some time each day looking at things around you and asking yourself, 'If I had to paint that, what colour would I use?' For instance, turn on your tap. If you had to paint a picture of that, what colour is the water? Alternatively you could try and describe a scene as if to a blind person who has never seen any of it. For example, what does a tree actually look like? How does it move?

This exercise will show you that you don't really see things as they are, but perhaps as they were once presented to you, and you've never up-dated your view of them. You could also try this using a person you know very well as your subject – for example, your mother. How would you see her if you didn't know her? What do you think her aims and ambitions are?

Summary Part One

So, now you know what causes worry, stress and all those other unpleasant high arousals. I hope the following summary of the first five chapters will be useful.

We all have a mechanism in our brains which warns us of danger. For our purposes we are visualizing this as a sentry. Just as we're born with different coloured hair, different shaped bodies, so too we're born with different types of sentry. We have classed these sentries as one of three types, the highly alert and easily aroused sentry, the tea-drinker whose reactions are average, and the sleepy sentry who isn't aroused easily. A person's ability to become aroused depends on a combination of the type of sentry they've inherited and the way they've trained that sentry over the years. Anything new, different from usual, or previously found to be unpleasant will arouse the sentry. Whether it stays aroused depends on whether you tell it the sensations you're experiencing are enjoyable or not. If you tell your sentry they're enjoyable, the sentry will relax and you'll find the high arousal exciting. If you don't enjoy the arousal, you'll find it will take on one of the forms of anxiety.

The sentry tries to discover whether a different situation is potentially dangerous or not by comparing it with similar experiences in the past. It tries to select an appropriate memory window through which you can view the present situation.

Memory windows help the sentry to feel calmer because they introduce a certain degree of predictability to things, that is, you tend to expect things to be the way they were before. Memory windows with bad associated memories can colour your view of the present in a negative way. Memory windows with good associations can give you a positive outlook. Whatever the situation, the memory window chosen may not be appropriate and may prevent you from seeing things as they really are.

The sentry is reassured by predictability. Predictability brings a sense of control. A feeling of loss of control results in greater rigidity of outlook and behaviour in a misguided attempt to regain control. This creates more anxiety . . . and so on.

Contentment comes from controlling what can and should be controlled and not trying to control what can't and shouldn't be.

> God, grant me
> the serenity to accept the things I cannot change,
> courage to change the things I can,
> and the wisdom to know the difference.
>
> Prayer of Serenity

PART TWO

Dealing Positively with
Your Feelings

CHAPTER SIX

Patience, Persistence and the Calm Reservoir

If it's so easy to overcome worry, and so good for us, why don't we all do it?

The answer to that is – because it isn't easy. At least, not to begin with. Most of us have spent most, if not all, our lives practising our bad habits. We couldn't abandon them overnight, even if we tried. Worry is one bad habit that society seems to encourage us to have – as I shall show later in this chapter.

In this second part of the book we're going to consider ways of bringing this change about. But first a word of caution. Remember that unfamiliar ideas, as well as unfamiliar situations, can arouse a highly alert sentry? Well, the fact that you're reading this book at all suggests that your sentry is probably of that sort, that is, you tend to become anxious easily. Therefore, to begin with, trying to change your present habit of worrying, unpleasant as it is, may make you anxious or uneasy, but you can minimize it. To begin with don't try to change. First, allow yourself to simply consider the possibility that you may change a little in the future.

As you get used to the new ideas, you can then begin to think about putting them into practice – we'll see how in the following chapters. For now, if at any stage whilst reading this book some of the ideas make you uneasy, leave it for a while to give your mind time to get used to them before continuing.

Two characters it is necessary to be acquainted with throughout all this are Patience and Persistence. We'll meet them in a moment. With their help anyone can do it – they only have to want to.

Wanting to is vital. Cures for such bad habits as over-eating and smoking never work in the long term on people who don't really, in their heart of hearts, want them to. Neither will half-hearted attempts to give up worry. Sometimes they may work for a while, until the novelty wears off. Then the relapse occurs and the cure is blamed as being of no use.

The fact is that no cure for such habits will work without the patient persistence of the person involved. There are no *magic* answers – but there are answers.

Giving up worry, however, does have one advantage over trying to stop smoking or over-eating – you're trying to stop doing something which isn't very pleasant. Thus, unless you're a masochist, your heart and mind should be willing. Once you've stopped worrying, guilt and stress will take care of themselves.

Giving up worry can't be rushed. Not for nothing are Patience and Persistence essential companions throughout. Patience will encourage you to take things very slowly, mastering one thing before going on to the next. Patience will keep you calm as Persistence urges you to keep on trying when things don't work out exactly as you expected the first time, or even the second, or third . . .

After all, as we've seen already, worriers tend to have obsessive tendencies. These can now be used positively, directed towards trying again, rather than being channelled into anger at yourself for not having got it right the first time.

You'll get to know Patience better as you spend more time with her. To begin with she's hard to stomach, but she grows on you and becomes a real friend.

Giving up worry reminds me very much of making gigantic snowballs as a child. It would start with a handful of squashed snow, that frequently crumbled before I'd even begun. Persistence would coax me to try again with another handful, Patience to mould it carefully. Eventually a small snowball would prove strong enough to withstand being rolled along the snow-covered ground. As it rolled it grew bigger and firmer. As it grew, I no longer needed the help of Patience or Persistence. I could do it myself. The snowball would roll downhill all by itself and end up so big and strong that I could stand on it.

When your attempts at overcoming worry crumble in the early days – picture my snowball. You can do it in the end if you keep your goals in mind, keep Patience and Persistence beside you, and don't let impatience distract or divert you – it can only get easier.

Persistence will help you here. Persistence is strong and determined. Persistence, however, doesn't waste effort. He directs his energies where he knows they'll be most effective. He doesn't waste his energies in anger or wishing things were different. Persistence gets on with it, calmly and with determination. Persistence knows where he's going and keeps going in the right direction, no matter how slow the progress or what the difficulties he meets on the way. Take him with you.

These then will be your companions. Create a picture of each of them in your mind. Look to them when the going gets tough and ask yourself seriously if you're following their example. The use of images is a very powerful tool, as is explained further in Chapter 9.

Now let us begin our journey by looking at those people who don't worry so much. Why are they less prone to worry than the rest of us? Probably for one or more of the following three major reasons:

1. Heredity

They're born with sleepy sentries and so generally become aroused less easily.

No solutions to be found here. Although you can change what you're born with, these people don't usually want to.

2. Familiarity

They have easily aroused sentries but have come across a particular situation before. Thus their sentries don't regard it as new, they've learnt what to expect from it and so it doesn't arouse them unduly or cause great anxiety.

You know the sort of thing – you feel very anxious on your first day in a new job, learning new routines, meeting new people, and so on. Gradually, however, as time goes by and the routines and faces become familiar they no longer arouse your sentry.

Time has always been recognized as a great healer of the emotions, because in time the person becomes accustomed to the change that has taken place in his or her life. The sentry adapts to it. Bereavement is a good example of this.

It is generally accepted in our society that a bereaved person needs time to come to terms with their loss. A bereaved person may show many of the symptoms associated with a depressive illness, but isn't treated for this because the cause is an acceptable one. Only if time fails to bring about an improvement is the depression viewed as treatable.

Studies of the bereavement process have identified seven separate stages. It is thought that each stage has to be passed through in order for 'recovery' to take place. Different people may take different lengths of time to pass through the various stages, but each stage will still be encountered. If a bereaved person fails to show the usual signs of passing through this process, concern is shown that they aren't grieving as they should.

These seven stages can also be applied to other great changes in a person's life, such as sudden redundancy, or loss of a limb, for instance. In fact, any change which is going to make an appreciable difference to the way the person sees him/herself – a change in self-image. Thus it might also be loosely applied to the individual who changes the habits of a lifetime.

I shall, therefore, outline these stages, relating them to

giving up worry. As with everything else, however, progress can't be rushed.

Stage 1 – a sense of being overwhelmed. This stage may not be very noticeable in the giving up of worry. On the other hand, simply reading this book may induce it. You may decide not to bother because it seems harder than you thought.

Stage 2 – the person tries to back up, tries to pretend nothing's happened. What's really happening here is that progress is being held up for a while. This stage is a means of biding time until the sentry comes to terms with the new ideas. As I said at the start of this chapter, don't push ahead until you're ready.

Stage 3 – depression. The person sees the situation for what it is and becomes depressed at the enormity of the task ahead. This is the stage at which people may give up if Persistence isn't with them.

Stage 4 – accepting reality. This is the point at which many people become stuck. They've realized what they have to do but can't seem to do it. This is the point at which letting go of the past occurs, the present is accepted for what it is and steps are taken into a different future.

Too few people actually know how to live in the present and put it into practice. This is a skill that needs to be developed. For many people undergoing change, this stage is slow and laborious because they lack this ability. They tend to have to sit back and wait whilst their sentries slowly adapt to the changes instead of taking steps to speed up this process. From here on in, however, things get slowly better.

Stage 5 – testing out new ways of behaving, of living life, of thinking. Actually practising the new techniques.

Stage 6 – considering the results of Stage 5. Deciding what works best for you. Everyone has to discover for themselves how to progress.

Stage 7 – the person takes the new way of life as natural and makes it part of his/her personality. Thus, a worrier would by this time no longer consider themself 'a worrier', but someone who can cope.

There remains the third cause for not worrying to consider.

3. The Calm Reservoir

This is the third reason why some people are able to minimize the amount of anxiety they feel. It's the easiest to control and also the one that's open to everyone if they choose to use it.

Imagine (see Figure 6) that everyone has a reservoir inside them. This reservoir is for calm. The higher the level of calm in the reservoir, the more resistant that person is to anxiety of any kind. On the other hand, the lower the level of calm in the reservoir, the more vulnerable the person is to stress, worry, anxiety and so on.

The level of calm in the reservoir may change constantly. Any form of tension uses up some of its resources. In extreme cases, if a person experiences a great deal of unpleasant emotion and no opportunity to replenish the reservoir, the reservoir becomes empty and stress-induced illnesses result.

There's no need to become alarmed at this, however. The reservoir doesn't empty that easily and there are plenty of warning signs before things reach such a point. Unfortunately, all too often these are ignored.

So, what is the tension that reduces the level in the reservoir? Simply put, tension is caused by any emotion or situation which the person dislikes or feels negatively about. It may range from mild frustration or impatience to blind terror.

Rather than merely concentrating on what lowers the level in the calm reservoir and avoiding it, it is far better to aim at

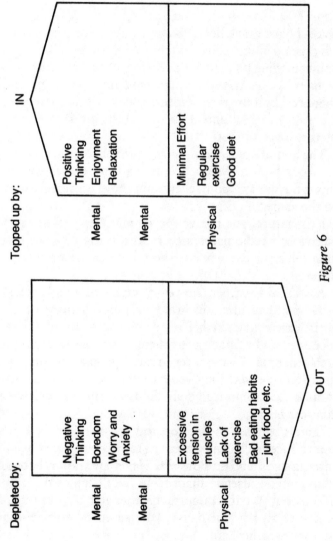

The calm reservoir

Depleted by:

Mental
- Negative Thinking
- Boredom
- Worry and Anxiety

Mental

Physical
- Excessive tension in muscles
- Lack of exercise
- Bad eating habits — junk food, etc.

OUT

Topped up by:

IN

Mental
- Positive Thinking
- Enjoyment
- Relaxation

Mental

Physical
- Minimal Effort
- Regular exercise
- Good diet

Figure 6

a way of life that constantly tops up the level in the reservoir. The following chapters suggest ways of doing just that.

HABITUAL ANXIETY

Before moving on there is one further cause for concern. Many of us have our naturally high tendency to become anxious enhanced by our environment. Unless we become aware of the ways in which this influence works on us, we can't take steps to overcome it.

The first of our surroundings which encourages us to worry is in our homes. Many people who are extremely anxious and who worry about everything have close relatives who do the same.

It is natural for the young of many species to copy the behaviour of the parents or those raising it. Thus it learns to survive, to eat what it should, to avoid predators, and so on.

As we saw earlier, however, much of man's instinctive behaviour has been distorted by modern living. Distorted to the extent that the behaviour copied by our children isn't necessarily what's good for them. Habitual worrying is one such example. I have often treated people for anxiety who have told me that they want to change as soon as possible because they've noticed their child beginning to behave in the same way.

This is not an excuse for you to say, 'Oh well, it's my mother's/father's fault then. I can't help it.' It isn't that important where or how you developed your habits, and whoever you learned them from didn't inflict them on you deliberately. What is important is that you, in your turn, don't inadvertently pass them on to younger members of the family. And you *can* help it.

Not only did many of us pick up our worrying habit from our parents, it's also fostered by the society in which we live.

Remember the story of Mary that I told in Chapter 1. In

response to my question, 'Why do you worry?', Mary said, 'I have to worry to show I care!'

I have posed this dilemma to several groups of trained nurses who've been attending courses on stress management. When we reached the point at which they agreed that worry was pointless, I asked them what they'd think if a relative of a critically ill patient under their care didn't appear worried on visiting. Almost without exception they chorused 'I'd think they were uncaring, unfeeling,' and so on. But why? Why does our society insist on an outward show of worry as evidence of an inward caring? The answer is simply that it's because that's what we've come to expect. This expectation is kept alive because we all go along with it.

This 'brainwashing' is done very subtly.

Recently there was a toothpaste advertisement on television which showed a mother waiting in a dentist's surgery, worrying in case her child had to have a filling. The hidden message behind the words was that, if you care about your child's teeth, you should worry in the dentist's.

We all go blindly on, fostering this unwritten law that we must worry to show we care, or to indicate that we realize a particular situation should be taken seriously.

When I had a lecturing job I would, as exams approached, venture to teach the students some good techniques to help them. One of these involved suggesting to them that, instead of standing outside the examination room beforehand trembling with worry, they try telling themselves what fun it would be and to look forward to it. The looks of horror and disbelief that this suggestion met with never failed to amuse me. You'd think I was suggesting they commit murder!

In fact, I was simply proposing they dared consider the idea that doing the exam might be fun. After all, when you're standing outside, waiting to go in and do an exam, it's too late to worry about what you may or may not have learned. In fact, the more anxious you become at this stage, the greater your chance of being unable to remember what you do know. Nevertheless there was this superstition among the students that maybe enjoying the exam was tempting fate!

As we saw in Chapter 2, the sentry records those times when you've experienced *unpleasant* high arousal. The next time you find yourself in a similar situation, that anxiety is reproduced. If, however, you consider the arousal as pleasant by telling yourself that what you feel is excitement not anxiety, the sentry won't record it and won't reproduce the feelings as a warning on another occasion.

Therefore, the more times you feel anxious outside an exam, the more likely you'll feel the same the next time, and the next, and so on . . . Whereas, the more positive you can be, the more chance you have of developing a positive memory window about exams and the more chance you have of actually learning to like them – and even look forward to them.

We talk of 'tempting fate' if we allow ourselves to be too optimistic. To think you're 'tempting fate' by enjoying something you've grown up believing you shouldn't only makes life harder to cope with. There's no reason not to enjoy everything. Only when you find yourself enjoying something you feel is indecent or morally wrong, ought you consider whether you should be doing it anyway!

This habit of not enjoying certain situations for no reason other than habit even extends to children, as my own daughter demonstrated to me in the following incident when she was nine years old.

She had to have some teeth extracted to make way for others to grow. These extractions were done over three visits to the dentist. After the performance she gave at the first visit, screaming and crying, I worked hard on her to reduce her anxiety for subsequent visits. The treatment worked well. So well that, on the third occasion, in the waiting room she said to me, 'Mum, I'm worried.'

'Why?' I asked. 'You know what to do. You know it won't hurt . . .'

'It's not that,' she protested. 'I'm worried because I'm not worried and I should be!'

Returning to the problem of Mary in Chapter 1: her lifelong insistence on worrying about everything had not only put her health in jeopardy, it had deprived her of the opportunity to be of any real use to those she worried most about – her family. The family had been warned by their GP not to tell Mary any of their problems so she wouldn't worry and raise her blood pressure. Mary, however, could sense when something was wrong and worried anyway.

She improved with treatment after being made to see that her worrying was simply a bad and unproductive habit. Worry also uses up the calm in the reservoir. A habitual worrier could be daily reducing the level, letting the calm trickle away. Then, one day, when a real crisis arises and the reserves are needed, there isn't enough there.

Worry is a futile occupation. If something is bothering you the first step is to identify exactly what it is. The second step is to ask yourself if there is anything you can do to improve the situation. If there is, you do it. If there isn't, you accept it.

This, in a nutshell, is the way to stop worrying. The following chapters tell you in more detail how to go about it.

Before you can stop yourself worrying, you have to be aware of when you are. To some of us the habit is so ingrained that we aren't fully aware we're doing it.

This is where Patience and Persistence come in. Persistence to help you keep trying, to keep you looking for those slips into your old ways. Patience to help you remain calm and not become angry or upset at your slow progress. If you can do this, you *will* change.

Many centuries ago, St Augustine of Hippo talked of the paradox of faith. He pointed out that people who said they'd believe in God *if* they first had some kind of proof He existed were going about things the wrong way. Faith means taking something on trust, without proof. St Augustine maintained that the reward for those who did this would be the evidence they sought.

In treating those who are over-anxious I often find myself echoing these sentiments. Patients all too often seek reassurance that if they do what I tell them it will work and they'll overcome their problems. Sometimes they'll half heartedly attempt what they're told and then give up because a miracle didn't transform them straight away.

It doesn't work like that with anxiety. You have to trust that it will work and let go of your anxieties *before* you begin to feel better. Anyone can do it – even you, if you take Patience and Persistence along as companions.

EXERCISE ONE IN POSITIVE LIVING

In the spaces in Figure 6, p.77, note particular small ways in which you will aim to change your own thinking habits so as to keep your calm reservoir topped up. Note these in the 'mental' section. We will deal with the 'physical' section after Chapter Seven.

CHAPTER SEVEN

Physical Calm

It never ceases to amaze me that so many people fail to realize that their bodies and minds are linked together. They behave as if the two are completely separate. The common view is to think of the mind as the computer that controls the body – and to some extent this is the case. But that's not the full story.

The body also affects the mind. This is not the case with computer controlled machinery. There, if the computer breaks down, the machinery stops. If the machinery gets dented, the computer goes on working provided none of the essential wiring has been damaged in the process. If the body becomes damaged, however, this information affects the mind.

We are not yet certain of precisely the ways in which the two interact. Most of us accept that if we injure our bodies, our minds don't feel as energetic as usual. On the other hand, we fail to realize that the power of our minds can not only impair the performance of our bodies, but that the power of the mind can also help the body repair itself when damaged.

Mental well-being is greatly assisted by a fit body. If you live inside a body whose muscles have forgotten what they are for, whose heart and lungs rarely get exercised or which get filled with cigarette smoke, whose skeleton has to constantly heave around a far greater load than it was designed to, a body which is regularly fuelled with inefficient or even poisonous substances – is it any wonder that the level in your calm reservoir is low? Its reserves are constantly being used to counteract the ill-effects of all the above, leaving little over to combat stress and anxiety.

If this is a revelation to you, don't panic. Don't suddenly try to change your lifestyle overnight – that isn't good for you either. You must change very gradually. If you are physically unfit you should consult your doctor before doing anything.

Before going into the next steps to take, I want to describe some of the many techniques which you can adopt in order to help you change. All the changes are aimed at living in such a way that you generally increase the level of calm in your reservoir rather than use it up unnecessarily.

The first step, therefore, isn't action. It's considering your present lifestyle in detail, with pencil and paper, and noting down all those areas which could do with some improvement. After reading through these next pages, you should have a better idea as to what these might be in your case.

I have divided the various means of increasing the amount of calm in the reservoir into two groups. The first group is dealt with in this chapter. It is made up of all those methods of topping up the calm reservoir that might be regarded as physical – they involve doing things to your body. The second group involves changes to make to your mind, your way of thinking. This group is described in Chapters 8 and 9.

If you can incorporate many of these topping-up methods into your routine everyday life, you'll be keeping your level of calm high and will be more resistant to stress and worry than you would otherwise have been.

Before we consider specific topping-up techniques, there are three adaptations to your everyday lifestyle that will pay dividends in terms of greater calm. These are exercise, diet and relaxation.

I can already hear you groaning inwardly as you recall having tried to give up bad eating habits in the past, and trying to stick to exercise routines. I don't mean that kind of thing. The type of changes I suggest have to be enjoyable in order to work.

EXERCISE

As you will recall from the first chapter involving Trog and the mammoth, some form of physical activity is the natural antidote to the emotional build-up of fear and anxiety. Physical activity tends to use up all those anxiety-related chemicals in the body. Hence, any regular physical activity of any kind is better than none.

In days gone by, before the advent of motorized transport, vacuum cleaners, washing machines and so on, many people, unless they were wealthy and had servants, had to do more physical activity to lead a normal life than we do today. These days there is a real danger that many of us will stop making enough use of the large muscle groups in our bodies – we'll forget how to move our legs for any distance, how to swing our arms and so on.

All you have to attempt to do in order to improve this aspect of your life is try to move more. You don't have to begin playing squash, join an exercise class, do strenuous workouts – although all of these can be most enjoyable and very beneficial to those who *want* to do them. All you have to do is walk up the stairs instead of taking the lift, move your body more as you clean the house, walk to the next bus stop before catching the bus and so on.

The important thing is that you enjoy the activity. Unless you're physically unable for some reason, everyone should aim to increase the amount of walking they do by just a little each month. Feel the ground under your feet, notice how it feels to really stride out for a few steps (see 'Tiger Walk' below, p.89).

Of course, if you're more ambitious you could take up swimming, cycling, riding, or some other activity that appeals to you. The secret is to find some time in your regular schedule where you can fit in ten minutes or so of such an activity on a regular basis.

I used to go swimming three mornings a week for ten minutes at a time at eight o'clock in the morning. I'd do my sixteen lengths, then get dressed, go home, and get the children off to school. I used to feel very much better for it. Swimming in a relaxed manner would calm me, make me more positive, make me feel healthier and more alive.

Just think about your lifestyle and find one small space where you could do something physically active for ten minutes or so, about three times a week. Don't be over-ambitious. Aim small and you'll be able to keep it up. Aim too high and the activity will soon become a burden rather than a pleasure.

DIET

The second general area for improvement is diet. Again, I'm not saying you must stop smoking or drinking or eating bad foods. The secret is to work on improving one small aspect of your eating habits at a time. For instance, you could have one alcoholic drink less each day, replace the white bread at one meal with brown, eat chocolate on fewer occasions, and so on. The overall aim is to eat more natural foods and fewer junk foods and alcohol. The aim is not to abandon the junk foods completely *if* you still enjoy them.

Anxiety tends to be exaggerated by eating lots of sugary foods, such as cakes and chocolates, and by alcohol. Unfortunately, these are often the very things we feel driven towards when we're worried – the comforters.

Although alcohol blunts the emotions at first, once the initial effect wears off it makes you more anxiety-prone and jumpy than you were to begin with. Unfortunately, many have found that the quickest cure for these withdrawal symptoms is more alcohol, the hair of the dog. Such solutions frequently lead to alcohol dependence.

Too much sugary food has the same effect. It raises your spirits to begin with but can lead to a craving for more of the same, at the expense of eating food that your body really needs.

The gradual development of good eating habits, therefore, is yet another way of keeping the calm reservoir topped up.

RELAXATION

A third general way is to practise some form of relaxation or meditation. This is especially good for those who, for one reason or another, can't do physical exercise. There are many commercially prepared tapes on the market which teach relaxation techniques. Alternatively, you may be able to relax yourself simply by listening to your favourite music.

Whatever it is, you should try to give yourself at least ten minutes' worth a day when you know you can let go and relax, and not be interrupted by anyone or anything. There's no point trying to relax totally while waiting for a phone call or when you expect to be interrupted. During this relaxation you should aim to let all the muscles in your body become as loose and heavy as possible. Sometimes it works best when preceded by a muscle tensing technique such as 'mattress pushing' (see below, p.93).

RESERVOIR TOPPING-UP TECHNIQUES

Where the specific physical methods are concerned, these can be divided into three groups. I have entitled these groups 'all the time', 'odd moments' and 'emergency'. We will consider the groups one by one.

1. All the Time

There is only really one technique in this group – but one that you should aim to make so much a part of your everyday life that it becomes as automatic to you as breathing. The name I give this technique is 'ME'. The letters stand for 'Minimal Effort'.

Think for a moment of what happens to your body when you become anxious or worried . . . Your muscles tense up, don't they? . . . As you read this, notice the muscles in your jaw and forehead – they're tense, aren't they? I bet that if you make a deliberate effort to loosen them up, to let them go, you'll feel a difference? . . . Did you?

We tense the muscles in almost all parts of our bodies most of the time – and it isn't necessary. When we're especially tense we don't even relax them in our deepest sleep. This results in people complaining of poor quality sleep, insomnia and so on.

Sleep follows a pattern, goes through certain stages. The first involves a relaxation of the muscles. If someone is so tense that they resist the natural tendency of the muscles to relax, then it stands to reason that insomnia will be the result. Also, people who learn to relax more are able to fall into the deeper stages of sleep quicker. The result is that they often need less sleep yet feel more refreshed by it.

What happens to your leg muscles when you try to walk faster because you're late? If you're not sure, make a point of noticing next time it happens. I'll bet they become tight and tense. As soon as we feel under pressure to achieve, we tense up.

But we shouldn't. Over-tensing impedes a good performance, it doesn't improve it. We can learn from toddlers. Watch a small child trying to walk. Although it falls frequently, it doesn't hurt itself unless it crashes against something, because it doesn't tense up as it falls. Skilled sports people have learned how to exert just the right amount of muscle power to do the job. If they tense too much, their performance suffers.

Each time you use more pressure than is required, tense a muscle more than is necessary, some of the calm in the reservoir is used up. It follows, then, that if you can only use the required amount, and no more, you'll be preserving more of your precious reserves of calm.

The way to train yourself is to day by day become more and more aware of times when you're using too much effort. Begin with one simple task at a time. I have found that the best tasks for beginners to practise are the following:

Teeth Cleaning – When you clean your teeth notice how hard you grip the stem of the toothbrush. Then make a deliberate effort to loosen your grip until you reach the point at which you can just control the toothbrush adequately. That's the correct effort required for that task. Everyone I've observed tends to grip the toothbrush far too tightly, and then tightens all the muscles in the forearm as well, not to mention the forehead!

Eating – Observe how hard you grip the handles of the knife and fork as you dine. As with the toothbrush, there's often room for improvement here too. You may have to tighten your grip on the knife from time to time to cut meat, but the grip should be relaxed again afterwards.

Driving – This is a minefield of excessive tension. A few months ago I treated a businessman for general anxiety. Part of his treatment was to carry out a general relaxation each day by listening to a tape.

A couple of weeks after starting the relaxation he came to see me in a state of amazement. The cause of this? Nothing more than the fact that he'd noticed the sensation of his fingertips against the palms of his hands as he held the steering wheel whilst driving. It transpired that whilst he'd been feeling generally anxious for years, he'd developed the habit of tensing all his muscles far too much. He'd been accustomed to clenching his hands tightly around the steering wheel. The pressure numbed a lot of the feeling in his sensitive fingertips. Once he learned to exert less pressure, however, the sensations in his fingertips suddenly became miraculously noticeable.

There are numerous small pleasures like this in life which the over-tense person is denied. Watch yourself. Do you grip the steering wheel too tightly? Do you tense your arm and shoulder muscles unnecessarily? Think of ME – Minimal Effort – and loosen up.

'Tiger Walk' – Watch yourself as you hurry around the shops or on errands. Are you tensing your leg muscles too much? Practise letting go a little and feel the difference.

I call it the 'Tiger Walk' after that magnificent beast in the petrol advertisements. Have you ever watched its rippling muscles as it bounds across the snow? Its movements are fast, yet smooth and flowing and beautifully relaxed. That's how I imagine my own legs feel as I walk around the shops – like the tiger's, loose and relaxed and swinging effortlessly from the hip.

ME then is the one physical technique for topping up your calm reservoir that you should use constantly. Don't make a big deal out of it. Don't become angry with yourself when you find you're too tense. Instead, as soon as you realize you're wasting muscle power, simply loosen up.

It's here that Patience and Persistence will be helpful. You may find that although you make an effort to reduce the tension in a particular set of muscles, before long they're tense again. Never mind. What do you expect when you've been training yourself to over-react for so long? Just keep patiently putting it right again ... and again ... and again ... Very gradually, over months and years, you'll find it becomes more and more natural to you. Some of the techniques described in the following two sections will help you initially to learn how to relax particular muscles simply and without effort.

2. Odd Moments

These are techniques which help you to train yourself to release groups of muscles easily and effortlessly. You should teach yourself how to do them and practise them in appropriate odd moments such as sitting in your office waiting for a phone call, watching TV, between courses in restaurants and so on. You can find other ingenious moments to use the techniques – moments which you'd otherwise have wasted.

Shopper's Relaxation – This is a technique for momentarily relaxing your entire body. Once you've perfected the technique you can do it anywhere. It's unnoticeable to those around you. I often do it in church during the sermon, waiting at the dentist's, while my hair's being cut, in a queue in the Post Office, on aeroplanes and so on.

All you have to do is to imagine you've just arrived home from shopping. You've walked miles carrying heavy bags in both hands. You arrive home, kick off your shoes, and sink into an armchair. Do you know that wonderful heavy feeling of relief that washes over you at that moment? This is what you're trying to imitate when doing Shopper's Relaxation. It's a brief state of total letting go of all the over-tired muscles. Your entire body should become absolutely heavy, dead weight, and loose and limp as you let out a deep breath.

If you're staying in the position for some time you can see if you can maintain the feeling by letting your limbs grow even looser and limper and heavier, right down to your toes and fingertips. You just have to imagine all the muscles loosening and relaxing. The skill improves with practice. You don't have to achieve a totally relaxed state in order to make some contribution to the reserves in your reservoir. The more relaxed you become, the greater the contribution. Don't, however, fall into the trap of becoming angry with yourself for not becoming as relaxed as you'd like, because that will lose you some of your precious calm. *Just accept whatever you can manage.*

Leg Flops – Unlike the Shopper's Relaxation, this one can't be done in public places – unless you're something of an exhibitionist.

I discovered that I enjoyed doing this very much quite by chance when I was little more than a child. As a toddler, my daughter caught me doing it one day and copied me. Ten years later she still does it.

I most enjoy doing this immediately after a bath while my muscles are warm and relaxed, but it can be done any time. Sometimes I use it as a means of working off negative thoughts.

This is best done lying frontally on a bed. It can be painful on the floor. Since I'm not very tall I lie across a double bed so that one edge crosses under my armpits. The tips of my toes don't extend beyond the opposite edge of the bed. If yours do, then you'll have to lie along the length of the bed, with your head and arms dangling over the foot of it.

You now bend your knees so that the lower parts of both your legs are pointing towards the ceiling. As you do this, try to keep the rest of your body as relaxed as possible, make sure your arms dangle loosely over the edge of the bed. Keep your chin, or side of your face, resting on the bed, don't lift it.

Now, you're going to allow your legs to drop back down onto the bed. You must do this without pushing them at all. Gravity must do it all for you. As your legs fall, they must be as limp as you can make them. You can judge how relaxed they are by the thud they make as they hit the bed; the more relaxed, the deeper the thud. Usually one leg will fall a split second before the other.

I often do this several times, enjoying the challenge of making my legs heavier each time.

Arm Flops – This is the same as leg flops, but can be done in more places. I often do it watching TV, or when I'm alone in a waiting room, for example.

The procedure is the same as for leg flops, but with the lower part of the arm. It's also easier to just do it with one arm at a time. Sit with the elbow supported on something soft. Raise the lower part of the arm so that it points towards the ceiling. Let the arm drop, letting it become as heavy as you can.

3. Emergency

This third group of techniques is particularly useful when you're worked up about something and want to calm down. They may also be used as general relaxation techniques at other times if you particularly enjoy any of them. The secret is to experiment in order to find out what works best for you and when.

Stair Running – Hopefully you will recall from Chapter 1 that physical activity is a natural antidote to anxiety. This is why Stair Running works. Sometimes when you feel very agitated over something it isn't easy to just sit down and try to relax; your body feels as if it wants to do something.

Stair Running is precisely what it says. Go and run up a flight of stairs. You may do this once, or more – depending on how long the stairs are and how fit you are. Afterwards, walk down the stairs and go and relax, according to one of the quieter methods.

Since you're then physically tired it's easier to begin to relax. You *must not* do Stair Running, however, if you're physically unfit in any way.

Mattress Pushing – This works on a similar principle to the above. You lie full length on a bed, either on your face or your back, whichever you find more satisfying. You then try to push yourself through the mattress using as many muscles as you can. You don't simply push down with your hands and knees, but, simultaneously, with your chin, chest, thighs, shoulders and so on (if on your front) or buttocks, thighs, calves, heels, shoulders, spine, and so on (if on your back).

Don't tense unnecessarily, but push down into the bed. You'll find that you catch yourself pushing hard with some muscles and neglecting others, and that when you turn your attention to these muscles, the original sets stop pushing.

This exercise not only helps you get to know the feel of different muscles, but also uses up some of your excess arousal so you'll then find it easier to relax. I find this technique is often pleasant if followed by leg flops. Again, watch that you remain calm as you do it.

Nose Breathing – This is a technique I adapted from yoga. It's fine done the yoga way if you're in a yoga class or somewhere private. It's not easy to do it properly on a crowded bus, or other public place, unless you don't mind people staring!

Since my aim here is to suggest ways of calming yourself

down in emergencies, it must be possible to do at least some of these techniques unobtrusively. Hence the modifications.

My version of Nose Breathing works firstly because it makes you concentrate on your breathing rather than on what's bothering you, and secondly because regulating your breathing calms the body's anxiety reaction. If you're in a public place, it's quite easy to disguise what you're really doing by pretending you're wiping your nose.

Throughout the exercise, try and keep the rest of your body as heavy and relaxed as you can. Take your handkerchief, or tissue, and hold it over your nose with your thumb and forefinger. Press on one side of your nose so that one nostril is open and the other closed. Breathe in through the open nostril for a count of four. Then pinch both nostrils gently for a count of four, holding the breath. Make sure you don't hunch your shoulders at this point. Next release the closed nostril and press the other one closed. Now breathe out slowly to a count of four. Then remove your hand and do nothing, neither breathing in nor out, for a count of four.

You then repeat the entire process beginning with the other nostril (see Fig 7). Don't worry too much if strangers appear to wonder what you're doing – it's only curiosity. They'll probably conclude you've got a heavy cold and you're trying to stop yourself sneezing.

A simplified version of nose breathing that can be used to good effect at any time is *counted breathing*. To do this you let your body grow heavy and breathe in deeply and slowly through your nose so that the air fills both your chest and stomach. It's nice, if you can, to rest your palms on your waist at the front as you do this. When you do it correctly, you'll feel your hands rise and fall as you breathe in and out. As you breathe in, you count slowly. Whatever number you reach, you MUST reach the same number, counting at the same speed, as you exhale.

Yet another variation on this is to do the counted breathing with your eyes closed and imagine you have a large coloured balloon inside you. As you inhale, you 'see' the balloon grow larger, and as you exhale, it deflates again. Decide what

Figure 7: SEVEN STEPS TO NOSE-BREATHING

1. Close left nostril by pressing side with finger.
2. Breathe slowly in through right nostril to a count of 1 – 2 – 3 – 4.
3. Pinch both nostrils between thumb and forefinger and hold for a count of 1 – 2 – 3 – 4.
4. Close right nostril by pressing side with finger.
5. Breathe slowly out through left nostril to a count of 1 – 2 – 3 – 4.
6. Release both nostrils, but don't inhale or exhale, for a count of 1 – 2 – 3 – 4.
7. Repeat entire process slowly and calmly until you feel relaxed.

colour, or colours, your balloon is and picture it as vividly as you can.

Do any number of these breaths you wish – the more the better.

These then are the physical techniques. I suggest you try them all at some stage. You will learn for yourself which you find most useful. You may find yourself using some of them a great deal and others only occasionally – it's your choice. Above all you must have Patience. Nothing works instantly. To give you an example of the need for Patience, I will tell the story of Kristine.

Kristine used to become so anxious that she experienced breathing difficulties and loss of vision. When this happened she became afraid she was going to die. Naturally, such thoughts only increased her anxiety and made her symptoms worse.

She'd been taught relaxation and breathing exercises, and understood that she was bringing the attacks on herself with her totally groundless fears that she would die. When she wasn't feeling anxious she could see how stupid she was. Nevertheless, when she worked herself up the next time, all her good intentions would go out of the window and she'd start pleading with everyone to tell her she wasn't going to die.

Afterwards she'd say about her attack, 'I know now that it's stupid and that I should relax, but I can't. I'm afraid that if I relax and let go I'll just die.'

It's at times such as these that St Augustine's observations about faith become relevant. In severe anxiety, when the natural inclination is to resist and fight, thus making the anxiety greater, you have to *trust* in what you've been taught – that *if* and *when* you let go, the fear will fade away. When you've done this once for yourself, you get your proof that it works. The *belief* that it will work, however, must come first.

Kristine tried to have this belief. She'd often attempt to relax as she'd been told – but she was impatient. Her symptoms would begin to subside, but she couldn't wait. She'd begin to check they'd gone. She was afraid she'd find they hadn't. This, of course, brought the symptoms back in a rush.

Where anxiety and worry are concerned, you have to have Patience. You have to persist in doing as you've resolved to do – especially when the going gets tough. It's at those tough times that your anxiety has got the better of you, not during the easy times.

Kristine eventually made it. Had she been friends with Patience earlier she'd have made it sooner. The ease with which most of us can make ourselves even more anxious by simply thinking shows how well-trained our sentries are to react to danger. You must always remember, however, that you're the sergeant-major. The sentry will do as he's trained to do, but *you* have it in your power to tell him to 'stand at ease'.

EXERCISE TWO IN POSITIVE LIVING

In order to decide the *physical* ways in which you're going to protect your calm levels, do the following:

1. Make separate lists of all the good and bad aspects of your life at present in this context.

2. Decide what changes you have to make and list these.
3. Rearrange these changes into some order of desirability
   – which do you want to tackle first? There's no right
   or wrong choice here, it's a personal one. There's no
   point in choosing something, such as giving up smoking,
   just because you feel you should, when you don't really
   want to. That will be a sure way to fail and you'll end
   up throwing away the entire project on account of it.
   Instead, first change those aspects which are easiest to
   change and/or which you most want to change.

   Over a period of time, as you grow generally calmer and
   healthier, you'll find it easier to abandon the others. I've
   known heavy smokers and drinkers who eventually began
   to lose their own desire to do these things because it no
   longer felt right to them. There was no anguish, no feeling
   they were being deprived of something they enjoyed. They
   reached a point where they preferred to feel healthier.
4. Begin by working on the item at the top of your list.
5. At the same time as trying to change one negative aspect,
   try to adopt one positive new technique. For instance,
   if you're trying to stop eating white bread and begin
   eating brown, you might also practise some arm flops
   each evening.

This is a suggestion. You make your own programme. Be
persistent, stick to it and enjoy it. Patience will bring your
rewards.

Write the physical ways you're going to keep your calm
reservoir topped up in the spaces on Fig 6, p.77.

CHAPTER EIGHT

Mind Matters I:
Facts and Feelings

Do you recall that in Chapter 5 we saw how memory windows can colour our views of the present and prevent us reacting to the situation as it really is?

We live our lives according to the beliefs we hold. Many of these beliefs are kept alive because we keep interpreting similar situations through those very memory windows which were created by those beliefs. That is, once we have formed an opinion about something, we tend to see other matters connected with it in those same terms. We don't generally approach a new situation with a totally open mind, or even a positively skewed one.

I've heard snooker players interviewed after a match in which they've made a particularly crucial shot. All too often they say how terrible it was because all they could think of was a previous occasion when that same shot had been equally vital and they'd missed it!

Now, I daresay they'd made that shot successfully many times on other occasions. But the good old sentry, always on the lookout for unpleasant consequences in an attempt to get you to avoid them, gets them to look at this shot through the memory window which bears the imprint of the earlier disastrous failure. As a result, the player begins to feel slightly uneasy, if not downright anxious. The muscles tense, the heart beats too fast for a very steady hand and eye, concentration is drawn away from the shot and towards the possible unpleasant consequences – and all too often the shot is missed.

Since we all form beliefs and opinions on the basis of what's happened to us in the past, these too are influenced by our memory windows. Many people are less than happy in their lives because they are viewing them through inaccurate sets of beliefs.

The American, Albert Ellis[4], in his many years as a psychotherapist, identified three very common mistaken beliefs of this kind. We'll call them *misbeliefs*. Ellis called his three the 'Irrational Trinity'. These were misbeliefs and opinions held by large numbers of his patients and assumed to be correct. They were never questioned by the patients concerned. But those patients were living lives on the basis of these same misbeliefs.

In the course of my own work, especially that concerned with anxiety treatments, I have also frequently come across those same misbeliefs. I have, however, discovered variations. My own Top Three Misbeliefs are as follows:

1. I SHOULD be worried about whatever, or it means I don't care.
2. I SHOULDN'T be too optimistic or it's tempting fate.
3. I SHOULD be liked by everyone.

How many of these beliefs do you hold? We've already touched on the first two. What are the implications of the third?

Have you ever been to a party where a person you've never met catches your eye? This person is noticeable for sheer strength of personality because they really seem to express themselves. You may or may not agree with the views they hold, but you respect the person nonetheless.

On the other hand, at the same party is someone who holds misbelief number three – that they must be liked by everyone. In order to achieve this, the person has to be wary of saying or doing anything that will offend or displease anyone. They are so easy to get along with that they go unnoticed, so afraid to offend anyone that nobody even knows what their real thoughts and feelings are – if, indeed, they have any.

The fact is that, in this world, it isn't possible for you to be liked by everyone. No matter how hard you try, how inoffensive you are, how saintly ... someone will dislike you. With this knowledge then, which would you prefer to be – remembered because you make an impression of some sort, or totally overlooked?

In order to even attempt to be universally liked, you have to constantly squash any elements in your personality which may be disapproved of. Because different people like and dislike different things, this means doctoring your thoughts, feelings, and behaviour to suit each person you meet. So, what happens if you have to spend time with two people whose views are so different that you can't possibly please them both?

These are exactly the problems facing those who believe they have to be liked by everyone. It isn't surprising then that such people frequently suffer severe anxieties and lack of confidence. They don't know who they are. A sense of loss of control of their own personalities creeps in, unsettling the sentry, using up the resources of the calm reservoir, and leaving them anxious and overwhelmed.

If whether or not you feel pleased with yourself constantly relies on the reactions of other people – whether they like you or not, whether they approve and so forth – then you have no real control over your own happiness. As we know how important a sense of control over yourself is for calm, anyone who constantly tries to please everyone is doomed to failure.

Why can't you please everyone, however good you are?

To answer this we need to turn this question the other way round and ask, 'Why do people dislike one another?' The answer to this is, strangely, very simple – it's usually because they feel in some way threatened by that person.

FEELING THREATENED, FEELING ANGRY

The psychologist, George Kelly,[5] said that we see the world in terms of what's important to us. Thus the qualities you see in your sister may be completely different from those qualities seen in her by one of her clients in the beauty salon where she works. Your sister is much the same person throughout. It's just that you and her client expect different things from her, and see those things rather than others.

To take another example, your grandmother may have a secret yearning to do a parachute jump. This is something you and the rest of the family are totally unaware of because it doesn't fit in with your image of the frail old lady, so it would never occur to you to ask her about it.

When you meet new people do you ever pay much attention to their noses, unless those noses are something really out of the ordinary? I bet you don't. Not unless you yourself happen to have a complex about your own nose. Then you'd notice precisely the shape of other noses, especially the ones you wish you had yourself.

It's the same when you're on a diet. You notice exactly how fat or thin other people are. When you're not so concerned about your own weight, you don't pay that much attention to the weight of others, unless circumstances force you to.

Exactly the same thing occurs with emotions such as hatred or jealousy. Very often you dislike someone because you perceive in them similarities to someone who's hurt you in the past. You dislike other people because they have something you wish you had and you're jealous. You dislike others because you're afraid they'll deprive you of something you hold dear, a promotion, a relative, a friend, your privacy, and so on. You become angry with other people because, in some way, you feel threatened by them.

People have become deadly enemies, family feuds have arisen, simply because the major participants in the dispute took the other's anger personally. Angry interchanges shouldn't really be taken at face value because there's often a wealth of information left unspoken. As an example, here's a situation which arose between Tom, a patient of mine, and his neighbour.

Tom was erecting the foundations of something alongside the boundary fence between his smallholding and that of his neighbour. The neighbour came out whilst Tom was working and looked over the fence. Tom immediately began to think, 'What does he want?' He also feared the neighbour might be about to complain since they weren't in the habit of chatting.

The neighbour spoke first. 'What are you building?' Now, we can suppose that the neighbour was afraid Tom was going to build something that might be a nuisance. The neighbour, therefore, already felt threatened by Tom's actions and this showed in his manner as he asked Tom what he was doing.

Tom sensed the aggression behind his neighbour's words and reacted with anger as a self-defence. Tom replied, 'It's none of your business!'

Of course, this made the neighbour feel even more threatened because he was now even more convinced that Tom was hiding something. The neighbour became more angry and repeated his question. Tom became angrier in return. The matter ended up in court.

This is an extreme example, but it's a true story. The sad fact is that if Tom had seen through his neighbour's first question to the fear behind it, and reassured him, the whole unpleasant mess could have been avoided. Tom could have reassured the neighbour by simply quelling the uncertainty as to what was being built. Tom might have said, 'I'm building a house for chickens but I can assure you they won't cause you any trouble with noise or smell.' After all, they were living on smallholdings where keeping chickens was not out of place.

The point of this story is to demonstrate how each person makes the mistake of thinking that the other's main aim is attack. The real motive for each, however, is defence. Each man feels under attack, his sentry is aroused, and, in order to defend himself, adopts the 'fight' reaction. Thus, issues which might be resolved amicably can be blown out of all proportion.

EXPOSING MISBELIEFS

There is a variation on the misbelief of 'I should be liked by everyone'. This relates to our own expectations of the way we *should* perform in a particular role.

For instance, there are women who believe they should be perfect mothers, and feel guilty at not presenting their families with home-made cakes, etc. This is a role that advertisers have played on for a long time in order to 'persuade' women with such guilt complexes to buy their products. For instance, they show a 'perfect' mother feeding her family cakes fresh from the oven and then that same 'perfect' mother cleans her sink with 'Whito' scourer. Now, the mother who is watching and feeling less than perfect because she doesn't make her own cakes sees a way to redeem herself by buying 'Whito' to clean her sink. Thus sales are made based upon your tendency to be misled by what you think you *should* be.

There are also people who have certain expectations as to how they should do their jobs. Often these expectations are unreasonable and unnecessary. Take William's case as an example.

William was sixty years old. He was in middle management and only had five years to go before retiring. He believed that, as a manager, he should be having ideas of his own. Consequently, whenever someone under him suggested a way of doing something, rather than judging it worthwhile and going along with the suggestion William always felt he should suggest something better because his position demanded it. In reality, however, William was rarely able to come up with anything better. Nevertheless, he spent many frustrating hours trying. He would lie awake at nights thinking, to no avail. He spent much of his time feeling anguished and stressed.

When he came to see me I suggested we should examine

his basic beliefs and assumptions about his job, in particular the one that said he had to have better ideas than his subordinates. Under scrutiny, this belief proved false. It became a misbelief.

He was also encouraged to remind himself of the other positive qualities he had which made him a competent manager. He hadn't been promoted necessarily to *have* new ideas, but to implement them.

When I next saw him, William appeared to have made a dramatic change in his outlook on life and was enjoying it far more as a result. He told me he had decided not to waste his energies trying to better perfectly good ideas, and creating futile worry for himself in the process. Now he said, 'I just let them do the work and go along with it.'

To an outsider, nothing appeared to have changed because even William's old self had been forced to accept the subordinates' ideas eventually since he rarely came up with better ones. The only difference was within himself. He had accepted the way things really were.

So, if you can't rely on the reactions of other people to you for your satisfaction, how do you judge yourself?

Simple, you set your own standards, have your own expectations of how you behave, what you achieve — and you live according to that, regardless of what others think. If you find the majority of people whose opinions you value disapproving of you then you may have to rewrite your standards. But *you* set them and *you* change them. You do what you've decided is right. Do *your* best at what you do — that's all anyone can ask. Only *you* really know when you have done your best.

If you live with strong ideas as to how other people 'should' behave, you are constantly going to be proved wrong. This will also give you a sense of not being in control. If, however, you live with a more open mind, if you have ideas as to how people usually behave but accept that they may behave differently, then your own expectations will cover all eventualities. You won't be proved wrong. Hence you'll feel more in control more of the time, and calmer.

ACCEPTANCE AND CHANGING
INTERPRETATIONS

This brings us to the next stage, that of acceptance. Having realized what's distorting your own view of reality, having identified your own misbeliefs, you have to learn to accept the facts the way they are. William accepted his limitations in rapidly coming up with new ideas and freed himself to direct his energies in more rewarding directions. Before you can accept the facts, however, you must know what they are, how to find them.

Two women, unknown to one another, are walking up the same high street, on opposite pavements, one morning. The first is going to get married, the second is going to her husband's funeral.

The first almost skips along as she watches the clouds scurry across the sky in a swirling dance. She sees the group of children playing happily outside the sweet shop, their little dog joining in the fun with his barks. She breathes in the crisp cool air of the morning, and feels happy.

The second woman trudges on. She watches as the clouds roll ominously across the sky and hopes she's home before it rains. She sees the children playing silly games outside the shop and cringes at the din made by their wretched dog. She pulls her coat tighter around her and sighs.

The point here is that both women are in the *same* place at the *same* time. They both see and feel and hear the *same* things around them. The difference lies in their individual interpretations of what their senses are telling them.

It's our interpretations of life that cause us problems, not the events themselves. If we can learn to see things for what they really are, with an open mind, we stand a chance of changing our interpretations, a chance of seeing something better.

Just as my daughter, in Chapter 6, worried because she wasn't worried about having her teeth out, so too many people allow themselves to continue being upset because they consider that's the behaviour society expects of them under the circumstances.

I always advise people who convince themselves they should remain upset by a bad experience to try and let go of it by telling themselves that, had they been asleep at the time, it wouldn't have bothered them. It's not what happens that upsets you, but what you think about it.

In the course of my work I sometimes see people who've suffered head injuries in car accidents. They've usually been unconscious for some time after the accident.

The important fact here is that, although they've been fairly seriously injured, virtually none of them develops a fear of travelling by car afterwards. On the other hand, people who've been involved in the same accidents but who've only received minor injuries, or none at all, frequently develop phobias about car journeys afterwards.

The difference of course is that those who've become unconscious don't usually remember anything about the accident afterwards. Their sentries aren't aroused by fear at the time and so don't record the situation as one to be avoided as dangerous. Those who remember it all, and remember the fear and unpleasant high arousal, have programmed their sentries with the information that here is a situation to be avoided – hence the phobia.

To be afraid following a car accident, for instance, is a reasonable fear, but not a very practical one to have in our society. It's not easy to lead a normal life avoiding car travel. Thus, people who have such a fear often seek help to retrain their sentries not to react so strongly, to reprogram them.

Life is neutral, neither black nor white. We colour it with the feelings we attribute to it.

Things happen and, once they've happened, they can't be changed. None of us can change the past.

But, as we saw in Chapter 5, we don't remember the past in terms of facts, but in terms of our feelings about it. If we can therefore learn to look back at the past through different eyes, through an undistorted memory window, we may be able to change the way we feel about it. If we can do this, we can replace our memory window and change the past for a better one.

Confronting Guilt

It is a pointless waste of effort to feel guilt over something that's past. It gets you nowhere. All it achieves is a wasting of calm reserves. The steps to coping with guilt are very similar to those for worry:

1. Identify exactly what you feel guilty about. What is it you think you shouldn't have done, or said, or caused to happen? If you caused something you consider wrong to happen, how did you do it?
2. Review the incident in neutral terms. That's to say, write it down in factual terms only, removing all interpretation, all feelings.

    For instance, suppose you washed an expensive jumper belonging to your mother and it has shrunk. You feel responsible. The facts are that your mother asked you to wash the jumper. You followed the instructions on the care label exactly. The jumper has shrunk. You can't change that.
3. Now that you see the facts, what do you think you should do about them? Do you feel you must make retribution to your mother? This may depend on how much the jumper meant to your mother, perhaps, and whether she'd really want you to replace it, especially in view of the fact that she asked you to wash it in the first place and that you followed the instructions. If, of course, you know you didn't wash it with the care it deserved, then you'll maybe feel more inclined to reimburse your mother.

Whatever you're guilty over, you review the facts, then decide whether or not you ought morally to make amends, and whether you practically can. If you've destroyed something that can't be replaced, you may have to find some other way to make amends. If, however, you decide that it wasn't your fault and/or you can't make amends, you have to simply chalk it down to experience, learn what you can from it, and go forward to other things.

Too many people become stuck in the centre of the problem, caught in a time warp, where they feel guilty but don't really know precisely what about so they do nothing. Whatever the source of a guilt or worry you *Must* confront it so that you can move on past it.

As I said at the end of Part 1, you must learn to distinguish between what you *can* control or change, and what you can't and therefore mustn't try to. Generally speaking, those things that can be controlled are in the present, the here and now. We must try to live in the present as much as we can, and see it for what it really is.

The case of John, quoted in Chapter 4, shows that you can go wrong not only by trying to control what's not in your power but also by not accepting control for what is.

Remember, John had back pain and constantly sought medical help to relieve it, to no avail. Only when he finally accepted that the pain *was* within his own control did he make progress. Using self-hypnosis he eventually managed to rid himself of the pain. He was so successful in this that later, when a specialist finally did find a physical problem with his back, he was amazed that John didn't suffer pain from it!

There's one word in the English language which often indicates an attempt at controlling something that can't be controlled. That word is *should*.

The use of the word 'should' implies that you'd like to be able to control whatever it is, but you haven't actually got control. To use the word, 'should', therefore implies you're feeling frustrated, even if only to a slight degree.

Consider the following examples of uses of 'should'. When you've read them ask yourself how often you use that very same word in a similar context in your thoughts or speech. Resolve to stop doing so. Each time you catch yourself using it, rephrase it so as to really mean what you're thinking along the lines in the following examples.

'He/she shouldn't speak to me like that!' But he/she has. Your expectations of life are proved wrong, you feel frustration and some loss of control. You could have avoided this by thinking, 'I'd prefer it if he/she didn't speak to me like that but if they do I'll report them/calmly explain what behaviour is required/put it down to anxiety they're feeling/and so on.

The appropriate ending depends on the people involved and the nature of the situation they're in.

'I should be getting on with painting the hall!' But you're not. You must decide whether you're going to paint the hall now or not. If not, accept it and enjoy what you've decided to do instead. If necessary you can fix a time in your mind when you will paint the hall — and stick to it.

Too often people don't do what they should and do something else but then spoil their enjoyment of it because they're feeling guilty about what they're not doing. So they suffer twice. First because they're not getting done what should be done, and secondly because they're not fully enjoying what they're doing instead because of the guilt.

Make your choices clearly, and stick to them. Give whatever you choose to do your wholehearted attention.

Worry and Action

This brings us to worry and how to stop it. If you have a worry you must first ask yourself precisely what it is that's bothering you – preferably write it down. Until you've identified a worry you can't do anything about it. Once you know what the worry is, ask yourself if there's anything at all you can do about it. To take Mary's case as an example, she said she was worrying about her daughter's marriage and whether it was about to break up.

Mary's next step would be to ask herself whether she could do anything to prevent the breakup. It could be that the problem was that the couple never had enough time to themselves because of young children. Mary might then offer to look after her grandchildren, perhaps have them to stay for the night now and then. In which case she would take the next step in solving her worry – action. She'd arrange with her daughter for the grandchildren to stay.

Suppose, however, that Mary's daughter's marriage was failing for reasons concerning only the couple themselves. Unless Mary's daughter actually sought her mother's help and advice, Mary would have to content herself with the fact that here was one worry which she could do nothing about. She must then turn her attention instead to something else. To worry under these circumstances would be pointless. It would simply use up Mary's calm reserves such that, if her daughter did suddenly require her help, she might not be able to do her utmost.

This is why worry is futile. You identify a worry and decide whether or not you can take action. Worry is the state of indecision: the state where something's causing you unpleasant high arousal, but you're not sure precisely what. All too often worries, as with guilt, take a hold because the person just doesn't stop and work out what they are. The pitfall is to become trapped in that stage where you're anguished about something, but you don't really know what, so you don't do anything except use up calm reserves.

A common source of worry is whether or not you'll pass an exam. If you haven't yet taken the exam, you must concentrate your energies on studying effectively from day to day. Looking too far ahead at this stage can be mentally paralysing. If you've taken the exam and really think you may have failed, rather than just brooding until the results are out, take definite steps to consider what a realistic course of action will be if you fail.

LIVING IN THE PRESENT

So far in this chapter we've tended to concentrate on recognizing what not to do. How not to be misled by distorted feelings about the past. How to move beyond guilt and worries. How not to try to control what you can't.

Now we're going to be far more positive and look at how you must aim to live not only in order to reduce the likelihood of your becoming a victim of stress, but also so that you might enjoy life more. And the best news of all is –

IT ISN'T PAINFUL. IT ISN'T ARDUOUS
YOU JUST HAVE TO DO IT!

What do you have to do? The first task is

LIVE IN THE PRESENT

Living in the present doesn't mean being modern in your dress, your ideas, your way of life. It means being aware of here and now. I will demonstrate what I mean by this with the case of Julian.

Julian was in his mid thirties, married with two children. He'd trained in physics, doing a degree as a day-release student over a long period. After qualifying he worked in the engineering industry, applying his knowledge to the processes involved. He was eventually made a manager of his part of the plant.

Although he enjoyed his work, he used to suffer many anxiety complaints. He was very restless when not working. He used to arrive at his office early and leave late. He didn't have to do this. He said he did it because if he wasn't working he was thinking of work anyway and planning the jobs he had to do the next day, and so on. He never enjoyed family holidays because he used to feel very anxious the whole time.

As I got to know Julian, it became obvious that he never lived for the present. He'd strive to get something done within a particular time limit, and even before it was completed he'd be thinking how he was going to tackle the next task.

He'd arrive at his holiday destination and immediately start thinking about what the family would do the following day. Even eating his meals he'd rush because he'd have his mind on what he had to do next.

This type of behaviour is common – too common. Too many people are constantly one jump ahead of themselves. By definition, they can never experience the satisfaction of something well done because, by the time they actually finish anything, their mind has gone ahead to something else. Such behaviour leads to a sense of being driven by life rather than the feeling that *you're* in charge. Again there's the sense of loss of control which can creep up and cause excessive stress and anxiety.

How often have you heard people who've narrowly escaped death saying that at last they've learnt the value of life? People with terminal illnesses say that they live one day at a time, and seem content to do so.

There is a paradox here in that, in order to feel some sense of control over your life, you need to have routines, schedules of what you must do, to calm the sentry. These take away the unpleasant arousal created by the uncertainty of where you're going and what you should be doing. Such schedules are, however, finite – that is, they have an end. You know what you have to do each day and when you've done it you can sit back and do whatever you want. Julian's lifestyle never allowed that. His schedule was endless – and so was the stress he created for himself.

Do you recall Linda, the lady in Chapter 4 who became anxious after giving up work to bring up her baby?

Linda had given up a very structured lifestyle where she had had to stick to routines in order to get everything done at work and at home. Suddenly she found herself living according to the varying demands of a baby with great expanses of 'free time' at unexpected moments. She became anxious because it was different, her sentry never knew what to expect next.

Linda overcame her problem by creating and sticking to a fairly flexible routine in order to give her day some shape and some degree of predictability. This calmed her sentry, and once she felt calmer and more in control she was able to break the routines if she wished.

The secret of living life in the here and now is to *enjoy* whatever you're doing at the time. It's important to actually think to yourself something like, 'Ah! This is lovely!' Thus, if you have to do certain things, try and view them in some way that enables you to feel positive. For instance, I have a friend who prepares the wages each week for a small firm. She says she hates doing this. I tell her that her attitude only makes things worse.

If you *have* to do something, then you may as well accept the fact and perhaps *enjoy* it.

I told my friend to find some way of enjoying her task. She could make a list of all the pay packets and reward herself with a toffee as she ticked each one off as completed. She could, perhaps, listen to some of her favourite music as she worked. At all costs she mustn't keep putting off the task because then it would be like a cloud hanging over her whatever she did.

It's better to set aside a time to do it in advance and stick to it. If the task is prohibitively large, break it into smaller stages and enjoy completing each one.

Each of us has to find our own ways of accepting and perhaps enjoying everything. I say, perhaps, because some tasks may not be enjoyable in any way, but they must be accepted. I used to dislike washing up until I accepted it had to be done. Eventually I devised my most efficient system for doing it and now take great delight in accomplishing it when I have to.

To take another example, suppose you dislike going to the supermarket. Instead of thinking how much you hate it as you push the trolley round, turn your attention to positive pursuits. There are many little tricks to make supermarket shopping more enjoyable, and no doubt you can come up with others. You could have a contest with yourself to see how neatly you can stack the trolley, you could enjoy ticking the items off a list, you could arrange to meet a friend in the coffee shop afterwards and make a social occasion of it. If you resent the time it takes, find time when you wouldn't normally do anything else. For instance, my daughter has a ballet lesson from 6 to 7pm one evening a week. I have to drop her off and collect her. If I went home I'd have to come straight back out again, so instead I go to the supermarket. There's just enough time to whizz round before I meet her.

Sometimes, if I finish quickly I buy a magazine to read in the car while I'm waiting. Often I just listen to my favourite programme on the radio. I find waiting in the car is one of the few times I really listen to the radio – and I enjoy it.

Another place I've trained myself to enjoy is – and people hate me for this – the dentist's chair. I've acquired a fine collection of fillings throughout my life and decided long ago that there was no point in dreading the dentist. I found myself a dentist I could get on with and proceeded to allow my mind to drift off to pleasant places whilst receiving treatment. (There's more about this technique in the next chapter.) Consequently the memory window associated with going to the dentist is a pleasant one and the thought evokes no dread.

Small enjoyments throughout the days and weeks add up to a high percentage of total enjoyment overall. The challenge of life is to make positive as much of it as you can. To develop the habit of turning everything to your advantage. But not, I hasten to add, at the expense of others.

For example, if you have to go into hospital, there's no point lying there thinking about all the things you could be doing if you weren't there. If you've got to be there, accept it and make the most of it. Enjoy the good aspects – the freedom to lie and read novels, to just stay in bed and have your meals brought to you, and so on.

Don't, as so many people do, lie there and constantly tell yourself what the adverse aspects are. If you keep making yourself see the positive side to it, you'll feel reasonably good. If, on the other hand, you persist in rooting out all the negative aspects, then you'll feel as you deserve to feel – miserable.

There are two kinds of people in this world. There are those who wake up each day and think, 'Oh dear, I wonder what life's going to throw at me today!'

Then there are the others who wake up and think, 'Good morning life. What can I get out of you today?'

By now you know which you're going to be in the future, don't you?

The more you can accept whatever comes along and turn it to your advantage, the calmer you'll be. We all have to have some goals, especially long-term goals, but we must guide ourselves towards them rather than be driven by them. We also need realistic goals. We must each know our own capabilities and not waste our lives trying to attain the impossible at the expense of enjoyment. If, however, you actually enjoy wishing, then carry on. It's only harmful if it frustrates you.

I recently came across a story from Zen Buddhism that demonstrates perfectly the technique of making the most of life, no matter what it throws at you.

A man was out walking along the cliff tops one day. He was enjoying the walk, the warmth of the sun and the freshness of the air. After a while he happened to glance behind him where, to his horror, he noticed a tiger. The tiger was walking in the same direction some way behind. The man began to feel uneasy and quickened his step. Glancing back, he saw that the tiger had done likewise and was now a little nearer. The man walked faster still. So did the tiger. The man began to run. So did the tiger. It was now closing on the man with every bound. The man ran as fast as he could and, suddenly, found himself at the edge of a precipice. There was nowhere to run and the tiger was coming closer, and closer.

The man looked around hastily and his eyes fell upon a creeper, growing down the rock face. With a sigh of relief he started to climb down. When he was about halfway down he paused and looked up. There stood the tiger, peering down. Relieved, the man looked down. There stood a second tiger at the foot of the rock face. The tiger licked its lips. The man glanced quickly up again and saw that the first tiger was now casually chewing through the creeper. So there he was – stuck. His fate was imminent and certain. As he waited, the man looked along the rock face to the side of him. A few feet away he noticed a wild strawberry plant, its roots tenuously clinging to a small patch of soil in a crevice. The plant held one large, red, juicy strawberry. The man eased out his right hand, picked the strawberry, and enjoyed it!

I urge people to 'remember the strawberry' whenever they find themselves in what appears to be an impossible situation with no salvation. Accept where you are and look sideways.

You never know what might turn up. Too many of us would have wasted those last moments which the man on the creeper enjoyed because we tend to look for the way out of a difficulty by the same route we took in. The solution to the impossible is to accept it and look sideways.

> IF YOU'VE GOT TO DO IT,
> YOU MAY AS WELL ENJOY IT
>
> THERE ARE THINGS YOU *WANT* TO DO
> THERE ARE THINGS YOU *MUST* DO
> BUT, there are NO things you SHOULD do!

At this point we'll return to Calamity Jane and her diary, and to yours.

Look over what you wrote. How often have you adopted a negative way of looking at events? How often have you blamed circumstances, fate, or other people for what happened to you?

Look at what Calamity Jane wrote for Friday 13th (end of Introduction). For a start, she's viewing the events of the day through a memory window which expects disaster simply because of the date. She'll therefore see the bad side of everything and will tend to blame circumstances for things she could have prevented herself.

Let's re-write her diary in the neutral – just the facts.

1. She overslept
2. On the way to work she punctured a tyre through her own impatience.
3. Trying to lift the spare tyre from the boot, she laddered her tights. She left the car and caught a bus as she was late for work.
4. She phoned the garage, who delivered the car to her office – with the bill.
5. The canteen had no curry.
6. There was no hot water for a bath immediately she arrived home.

These are the facts. Now let's examine them through a more positive memory window.

Jane overslept. This at least meant that she caught up on some of the sleep she'd deprived herself of recently. Once she'd woken, she had only to do the minimum of chores before leaving so she wouldn't be late for work.

Driving to work she got stuck in a traffic jam. This meant she was able to hear more of the radio programme than usual. Had she accepted this situation calmly and made the best of it she'd have avoided the puncture. She ended up late anyway – and with a bill for the car!

The fact that there was no curry for lunch gave Jane the opportunity to try the lasagne instead. She'd often wanted to try it but had been reluctant previously to forego the curry.

On arriving home it was just as well the water wasn't hot because it gave Jane the chance to get on with the chores she'd neglected that morning.

EXERCISE THREE IN POSITIVE LIVING

1. Look at your own diary – the one you were advised to keep at the start of this book. Look at it in the same way we have just reconsidered Jane's.
   Re-write just the facts and then try and see them through a positive memory window.
2. Look back at your answers to 'Lesson Four in Understanding'. Do you see the worries in a different light now? If not, perhaps you should re-read this chapter.
3. Make a list of all the things you think you *should* do. Are they really *want to's*, or *have to's*, or neither?

LIFE'S NEUTRAL. IT'S OUR OWN THOUGHTS THAT COLOUR IT!

CHAPTER NINE

Mind Matters II: Techniques

Just as there were specific physical techniques for you to try in order to help teach yourself physical calm, so too there are mental techniques to help you teach yourself how to make your mind work for you rather than against you.

Most of these techniques involve the use of imagery. Imagery is making use of pictures, images, which you can conjure up in your head at will. The vast majority of us think and remember in pictures. We dream in pictures. If you've ever learned to study effectively, you'll know that the use of charts and diagrams help you to remember far more effectively than mere words alone.

Many memory techniques involve the use of images. For instance, there's one technique for remembering long series of numbers which involves associating each of the digits from 1 to 0 with an image.

Thus, 1 might be a bun, 2 a shoe, 3 a tree, 4 a door, etc. You'd learn this well. Then, when you wanted to easily learn a number, say 3424213, you'd simply visualize each of the images in turn, making some connection between them as you did. The more ludicrous the association, the better you'd remember it. So, for 3424213 you'd begin with a tree(3), and in the tree would be a door(4). Hanging on the back of the door would be a shoe(2). You put on the shoe and go through another door(4) where you find another shoe that doesn't match the first(2). You put on the shoe and step on a bun(1) then scrape it off on a tree trunk(3).

This is only a limited example of this type of memory technique. There are many excellent books on the subject if anyone's interested in taking it further. If, however, you imagined the pictures as you read, you should now be able to write down the number with a little thought. Such is the power of images when used to your advantage.

The first specific technique I want to describe is that of:

1. Positive Thinking

Approach this as a game. See how often you can catch yourself interpreting things negatively rather than positively. Remember, life is neutral. It's your interpretation of life that determines how you feel about it and the memories you have.

I once knew a lady called Margaret who had the art of negative thinking perfected. She could see the worst in any situation. She related to me the events of a royal wedding in terms of a poor little dog in the crowd that had its foot stepped on! Needless to say, she was a very unhappy person generally.

It costs nothing and harms no-one to look on the bright side – and it isn't tempting fate. Superstition has no place in positive thinking.

2. Thought Stopping

This is used when you've developed bad habits of thinking unwanted thoughts. Obsessional thoughts, or thoughts of doom or failure come into this category. It means that whenever you become aware that you're thinking these things, you immediately think the word STOP. As you think it, you flash the word, oddly written in warning colours, through your mind.

To make it more effective, you might picture the word STOP written across a huge balloon and as you read it the balloon bursts with a loud bang. The purpose of this is to divert yourself from the course of thinking you're indulging in and give yourself the opportunity to move your thoughts in a more positive direction.

You can use this technique for all kinds of thoughts. For instance, if you're stuck in a traffic jam and you find yourself impatiently thinking you're going to be late for that important appointment, you stop the thoughts, sweep them out of your mind, and replace them with more positive ones – relaxing thoughts, or working out a new plan of action for something, and so on. After all, when you're stuck in a traffic jam there's no point whatsoever in becoming agitated about being late. You're not in control of that, so accept the situation. But you are in control of your thoughts, so make them do something beneficial.

After the image of the balloon bursting you could even see a huge broom sweep the word impatience away, symbolic of clearing your mind.

It's often advantageous to use the 'Calm Scene' technique (below) in conjunction with thought stopping.

3. Calm Scene

Conjure up in your mind a perfect place. The calmest, most peaceful place you've ever been, or you'd choose to be. This might be seeing yourself walking along windswept cliffs at dusk, strolling through a summer meadow, sitting on a swing in a beautiful garden, lying on a tropical beach, or in a hammock ... The possibilities are endless and each person's ideal place is different.

My own calm scene is of sitting on one of those lovely padded swinging settees in a beautiful garden beside a stream on a warm summer's morning. I can feel the gentle rocking of the settee, feel the warmth of the sun on my skin, tempered by an occasional gentle breeze that just brushes my cheeks and ripples my hair. I can hear the birds and smell the air and the flowers. I can hear the stream gurgling gently . . .

I have practised imagining this scene so often that I can now conjure it up instantly. I bring it to mind momentarily when I feel myself begin to be unpleasantly aroused immediately after thought stopping. At other times, for example in the dentist's chair, I conjure it up, let my body go heavy and relaxed at the same time, and wallow in it.

It's not easy to do to begin with. You'll need to practise doing it when relaxing many times before it becomes so automatic that it will get past your sentry at times of stress. To begin with I suggest you practise as you lie in bed at night, as well as at times you've nothing particular to do, such as on the bus going to work.

4. Self-Hypnosis

Once you've learnt how to relax your body and conjure up a calm scene, you can begin to introduce all kinds of images for yourself so as to reinforce your willpower. This is, in effect, a form of self-hypnosis.

There's nothing mumbo jumbo or mysterious about hypnosis. It's simply a state of mind at which point you're able to achieve greater control of your own desires and feelings than you can normally. In many respects, the state of hypnosis is one which almost overrules the will of the sentry to arouse you. I say 'almost' because even under self-hypnosis you will still react to real, life-threatening danger.

A state of hypnotic suggestibility is reached when your mind is prepared to totally accept, without question, what you tell it.

Your mind has two parts, a conscious part and an unconscious part. When you're conscious, the things noticed by your senses – your eyes, ears, touch, nose, and taste buds – are all passed through your conscious mind for evaluation before being acted upon. Anything which seems unbelievable or impossible to your conscious mind is thus rejected.

For example, suppose you glance out of your window now and see a pink elephant. You won't simply think to yourself, 'Aha, there's a pink elephant outside,' and go on with what you were doing, would you? You'd rub your eyes and look again to check you weren't seeing things. If the elephant was still there you'd get up to see if it was a joke of some kind, or whether there was a circus passing by ... You'd have to find a logical explanation for its being there, or conclude you were seeing things.

In the same way, many suggestions we make to ourselves never get taken up because our conscious minds reject them out of hand. For instance, if I tell you that after reading this book you'll immediately stop worrying, you'll think to yourself that it's too good to be true and reject the idea.

Now, if the same suggestion were able to reach your unconscious mind, without having to run the gauntlet of your conscious mind first, it would be accepted as a real possibility and you'd begin to act upon it.

That's what happens under hypnosis. It switches off your conscious mind so that the messages are permitted to pass unhindered to your unconscious. The conscious mind is switched off by relaxation. As you relax you have to accept everything you feel without question. It's easier, therefore, to practise at first with a tape. It's easier to adopt a mood of acceptance if you don't have to think at all but simply follow instructions.

Once you've learned how to do it, you can drift off to your calm scene and feed yourself all kinds of thoughts to make yourself do what you really want to do and be the kind of person you really wish to be. The changes don't come overnight. But they're gradual and worth waiting for. Patience is very necessary.

Once you're able to take yourself into this calm, trance-like state, you can use all kinds of images. These are several I've found useful.

First, if you've got thoughts that won't go away, picture yourself writing each one on a large blackboard. When you've done that, read them for the last time before taking the board rubber and erasing them for good.

Another way for disposing of unwanted thoughts is to write each on a piece of paper, toss it into a stream and watch as the current carries it away. A variation on this is to toss pebbles, each one bearing an unwanted thought, into the sea.

As with everything else, the images you use are your choice. If they work for you they're OK.

As well as ridding yourself of unwanted thoughts and habits, you can also strengthen your resolve. You can, for example, come to increase your self-confidence by seeing yourself walking in the rain. Each raindrop that falls on you brings more and more self-confidence. The raindrops could also represent patience, or determination – whatever you wish. Alternatively you could gather these same qualities for yourself by picking up fallen rose petals until your pockets are full. Again, you can vary these according to your own imagination and preferences.

As I mentioned earlier, it's easier to learn to do muscle relaxation and hypnotic imagery to a pre-recorded tape. The aim of the listener is to abandon him/herself to the voice on the tape and to experience exactly what it says without evaluating or criticizing. Thus, if a tape tells you that your left arm feels heavy and relaxed, then, as far as you're concerned, your arm *is* relaxed, even if, in reality, it's rigid with tension.

5. Living

This is teaching yourself to see and feel more of what's around you. This is a means of enjoying the wonder of life more than most of us do. Most people are so busy rushing from one goal to the next that they fail to appreciate much of what's around them.

You must make yourself more aware of the input to all your senses. When did you last really notice different textures beneath your feet as you walked along? Do you notice different smells – of freshly fallen leaves, of a spring morning, of freshly cut grass and so on? Do you notice the different colours and textures of the bark on the trees in the parks and gardens? Do you see the different colours of people's hair as you stand in the queue at the Post Office? What does water running through your fingers feel like when you wash your face?

Noticing some of these simple things helps to make you live in the present. There is much to be appreciated around us all each day. All too often we only become actively aware when we don't like something. Why not resolve to try and experience something new each day? All this encourages the positive habit which, in its turn, keeps the level in the calm reservoir high.

EXERCISE FOUR IN POSITIVE LIVING

In order to better appreciate the power of your own mind, I decided to include here a series of simple games to demonstrate to you your own powers of creativity. They're also good practice in patience and acceptance for those who need it. All these games have no right answers. You have to allow your mind freedom to create and have fun doing it.

1. Doodles – Most of us doodle and, when we do, our doodles almost always end up the same. In this exercise you try to doodle as differently from usual as possible. For instance, being a tidy person, my doodles tend to be balanced and have no loose ends. Sometimes I deliberately make myself draw doodles that aren't symmetrical and which have squirls and twiddley bits left over. The emotions aroused by this are interesting. It's also a good time to practise accepting.

2. *Poems* – This is when you write down any sentence that enters your head, then try to write a second line that rhymes, and so on. It's quite surprising the things you come up with.

3. *Free association* – This is well known. You start by writing down the first word that enters your head. Then you write one associated with the first. You then keep writing so that each word is associated with the one before it. It doesn't have to be written down, you could do it mentally whilst waiting in a queue.

It might be an interesting exercise to do a written version now and keep it somewhere safe. In some months time, repeat the exercise with the same start word and see how your thoughts have changed.

4. *Party pictures* – This version of free association is done with a group of people. It's done for each individual to enjoy their own experience. Nobody ought to be made to give their reasons for any association they make if they choose not to.

The participants sit in a circle and close their eyes. The game begins by one person saying a word. The person on the left then has to say a word associated with the first. The difference between this and straightforward free association is that as each person speaks their word they touch the hand of the person on their left whose turn is next. As each word is added the other participants must try and visualize it rather than just hearing words. After a while, provided the eyes are kept shut, the experience is interesting.

If there's one image you ought to be able to call to mind after reading this book, it's of yourself beside a beautiful blue reservoir, holding hands with Patience and Persistence.

CHAPTER TEN

Last Words

There's a lot to take in at once. I don't expect anyone to be sure of how to go about it after only reading this book once. Ideally you should read it the first time to pick up the gist of the message. Then leave it for a while so your sentry has time to become accustomed to the message. Then read it a second time, this time knowing where it's leading so you're able to apply the information to yourself as you read. Perhaps then attempt one or two of the simpler exercises. Finally read it a third time before beginning in earnest.

As I said at the very beginning when I gave my reasons for producing yet another book on worry, a person can hear the same information from many different sources but still not understand it fully. Often, on having it put differently, all at once the penny drops and the message gets across.

When he was small, my son proved this to me. He had to have an injection at the dentist's (where I find so much of my raw material!). He hated these and complained they hurt. I kept telling him that if he relaxed, the muscles in his mouth would slacken and the needle would go in far more easily. At least, I thought that's what I'd told him. But to no avail. He persisted in tensing up and complaining it hurt. Then, one visit, in desperation I demonstrated the principle using his own locked fingers as the tensed muscle. I told him to imagine my finger was the needle as I tried to force it between his clenched fingers. I forced 'the needle' through and it hurt him a little. I then told him to relax the 'muscle' by loosening and relaxing his fingers. This time I was able to push my finger through easily and painlessly.

He put this into practice and came out of the surgery later, a beam on his face in place of the customary tears. 'It worked, Mum!' he said. 'Why didn't you tell me to do that before!'

If there was a main message to this book it would be to learn to recognize when to accept things and when to control them.

Many people who've been involved in major accidents suffer a form of anxiety neurosis afterwards. Talking to them reveals that, for the large part, they're feeling angry that their life was taken out of their control and changed. They tend to feel that the accident shouldn't have happened to them and affected them as it had.

Whilst this reaction is understandable, and you'd sympathize with anyone who'd suffered in this way, the way forward is to accept that these things happen, learn anything from it that's to be learned, then put it aside and direct your energies to living positively. Unfortunately there's a tendency for people to feel that their accident won't be seen by others as having been serious if they're able to shrug it off easily, as in 'I shouldn't get better so quickly'.

RE-EVALUATE YOUR LIFE

Stress and worry aren't caused simply by doing too much – as the GP in the example given in the Introduction seemed to think. They're caused by seeing and feeling too much too negatively.

The woman in the story in the Introduction needed to re-evaluate her life. She needed to abandon anything she could which caused her unpleasant high arousal. Any such things that couldn't be abandoned, cooking for the family for instance, would have to be accepted and seen in a more positive light. She would also have to practise drawing her own attention to the more positive, enjoyable aspects of her life. In addition she could incorporate some of the topping-up techniques described here.

It's wrongly thought that workaholics will give themselves breakdowns and stress-related illnesses by virtue of the hours they work. A true workaholic won't. The true workaholic actually *enjoys* working and chooses to do so. The true workaholic doesn't feel guilty about working to the exclusion of all else.

It's so-called workaholics, driven to work long hours by the thought that they *should* be working although they don't really want to, those who keep working excessive hours because they feel driven by pressures other than their own enjoyment of the work – they're the ones at risk.

We each have to be honest with ourselves. To re-evaluate our lives and consider honestly what we have to do, what we want to do, and what we keep doing for no real reason. We must steer ourselves towards more enjoyment, less sense of being driven by outside forces.

We can all be more of what we want to be – we just have to allow ourselves to move towards it. It's not what you do, it's the way you think and feel about it.

Your life is here and now. This isn't some kind of dress rehearsal – *This is the real thing! Enjoy it! Don't let it slip by.*

Appendix 1

Is it Fear, Anxiety, Stress or Guilt?
(Answers to questionnaire at end of Chapter 1)

1. The answer is ANXIETY. You're experiencing unpleasant high arousal because you think you may not be able to answer all the questions tomorrow. On the other hand, you may be feeling anxious out of sheer habit.

   If there's any benefit in reading calmly through your notes for the exam, then do it. Don't attempt to learn anything new at this stage, however, because it will probably only confuse you. Read your notes, then forget the exam with a clear conscience and do something else – watch a favourite TV programme, for example Do so wholeheartedly and not with a guilty feeling that you should be swotting – you shouldn't. Tell yourself that tomorrow it will be over. You've got to do it and so you'll see how much you can remember when the time comes. If you know you haven't worked hard enough you must accept the fact and learn from it. Even if you fail, it won't be the end of the world. There will always be something you can do to make amends. In fact, it may prove to be the best thing that could happen. Look forward positively.

2. The answer is WORRY. It's your daughter who's taking the test, not you. You couldn't influence the outcome now no matter what you did. Relax and work out what you can say or do to comfort her if she fails. It's not the end of the world if she does. It might be nice for her to pass now but if she doesn't you must accept the fact that sometimes we learn more from failures than from success.

3. This is ANXIETY. You probably have a fear of heights which

you're transferring to the characters. Presumably, once the scene ended you'd relax again.

Most people with highly alert sentries (see Chapter 2) don't particularly enjoy those films which centre around some kind of large-scale disaster – such as *Inferno* and so on. They don't enjoy the suspense and chaos. Such films appeal to those with sleepy sentries who require such extreme situations in order to arouse their excitement. Think of the people you know who like or dislike such films. What sort of sentries would you say they had?

4. This is STRESS. If you're confronted with the possibility of something unpleasant you have to make some decisions. You have to do something. There's no point waiting to see what happens because this throws you into a state of non-control.

   Take charge of the possibilities. Consider realistically what you would do if you were made redundant. Face up to the possibility. If then the worst doesn't happen you'll be over the moon. If it does you'll be prepared.

5. This is FEAR. You anticipate something unpleasant is about to happen to you. It's fight or flight time. These need not be done physically. Since his car was stationary there's little chance that it wasn't your fault. He's going to be on the **defensive** because he's afraid you're going to try and avoid the responsibility. To defuse the situation you have to allay his fears by apologizing, giving your insurance details, and so on. There's no point in your becoming angry because he is: that will only make matters worse.

6. This is GUILT. In reality there's nothing you can do about the fact that you hadn't made your peace before the man died. You must learn from the experience and take what you've learned forward into the future. For instance you must tell yourself that in future you'll apologise immediately – you could, for example, have phoned him when you discovered your error – and not let time lapse.

Appendix 2

Answers to questionnaire at the end of Chapter 2 in Lesson
Two in Understanding

Your first day in a new job

This situation arouses the sentry because usually the place
you're working in is unfamiliar. The routines and other
people are unfamiliar, and the more unfamiliar aspects to
the situation there are, the more highly aroused the sentry
becomes.

The sentry can be calmed if someone new to a job doesn't
try and do too much all on the first day. Don't meet all the new
people at once, just get to know those with whom you'll be
most closely involved. Don't buy new clothes and wear them
for the first time on your first day. You'll feel more reassured
by clothes you're used to.

Dressing up to go to a wedding

As with number 1, the problem here is a combination of the
type of clothes you're not accustomed to wearing coupled
with the fact that you're going to meet a lot of strangers at
the reception.

Instead of dreading who might be there, look forward to
it positively.

Meeting new people

This is because you're concentrating on yourself. You're
wondering what other people are thinking of you, worrying

whether they'll like you, and so on. The trick is to forget yourself and concentrate your attention on others. Find out about them, show genuine interest, and you'll soon forget about yourself. Most people like a new acquaintance who asks them about themselves – providing the questions aren't too personal.

Embarking upon a course

The arousing aspect here is probably a combination of studying in the evenings, the topics you're studying, and the new people.

Most of us are accustomed to being taught during the day – a hangover from our schooldays. You just have to tell yourself all the good things about being taught at night instead. As far as people are concerned, the fact that they're doing the same course shows there's something in common. Ask them their reasons for being there. Be more interested in finding out about them than in wondering about the effect you're having on people.

Giving up work to bring up a baby

This involves a whole new routine and a change in self-image. The sooner you can establish a new routine for yourself the better. The trouble with giving up work is that people have too much unstructured time on their hands and they simply can't decide what to do with it. This indecision causes the unpleasant arousal.

You have to come to terms with your new role in life. There's no point in hankering after days gone by if you can't have them at present.

Retirement

The problems here are similar to the above. You have to establish new routines and a new self-image as soon as you can.

Illness in a member of the family

When someone in the family is ill it results in changes in routine for everyone else. Although the patient may not be seriously ill, simply the fact that they aren't at the breakfast table as usual can unsettle others. Things aren't the way they usually are and this arouses the sentry.

Be aware of this and tell yourself that things are bound to be anxious while so and so is ill, but they're on the way to recovery. When little things cause you unease, admitting it to yourself often takes away the unease.

References

1. Selye, H., *The Stress of Life*, McGraw-Hill, 1976.
2. Gray, J. A., *The Neuropsychology of Anxiety*, Clarendon Press, 1982.
3. Cohen et al., 'Psychological Stress and Susceptibility to the Common Cold', *New England Journal of Medicine*, 1991, Vol. 325, pp. 606–12.
4. Ellis, A., *Reason and Emotion in Psychotherapy*, Lyle Stuart Press, 1962.
5. Kelly, G. A., *The Psychology of Personal Constructs*, W. W. Norton, 1955.

Further Reading

For those who wish to continue to develop their ability to use their minds positively, I have listed below the titles of some books. None of these deal specifically with worry – but then you should know by now how to stop that yourself!

Buzan, T. with B. Buzan. *The Mind Map Book*, BBC Books, 1993.

Hay, Louise L. *The Power is Within You*, Eden Grove, 1991.

–, *Love Yourself, Heal Your Life: Workbook*, Eden Grove, 1990.

Koran, A. *Bring out the Magic in your Mind*, Thorsons, 1993.

McKenna, P. *The Hypnotic World of Paul McKenna*, Faber & Faber, 1993.

North, V. *Get Ahead* with Tony Buzan, BC Books, 1991. (This is a much simplified version of the above.)

Useful Addresses

Most learned and professional associations publish a directory of members. These directories can be consulted in major reference libraries. I have listed below some of the directories you might wish to consult to find a local practitioner. I have given the addresses of the major associations dealing with the practice of hypnosis.

1. BSECH – (British Society of Experimental and Clinical Hypnosis)
    'Westview'
    Westport
    Nr Langport
    Somerset TA10 0BH

2. BSMDH – (British Society of Medical and Dental Hypnosis)
    17 Keppel View Road
    Kimberworth
    Rotherham S61 2AR

3. BSH (British Society of Hypnotherapists)
    37 Orbain Road
    London SW6 7JZ

4. The Voluntary Agencies Directory (lists all manner of groups for all sorts of problems)

5. The Natural Health Yearbook (the who's who for natural healthcare organizations and professionals)

6. The Holistic Network Directory (the directory of holistic practitioners and centres in the UK and Eire)

7. Directory of European Medical Organizations

Those readers who live outside the UK are advised to consult relevant directories in their own libraries.

Index